THE SWEET POISON QUIT PLAN

DAVID GILLESPIE is a recovering corporate lawyer, co-founder of a successful software company and consultant to the IT industry. He is also the father of six young children (including one set of twins). With such a lot of extra time on his hands, and 40 extra kilos on his waistline, he set out to investigate why he, like so many in his generation, was fat. He deciphered the latest medical findings on diet and weight gain, and what he found was chilling. Being fat was the least of his problems. He needed to stop poisoning himself.

David is also the author of the bestselling *Sweet Poison*, *Big Fat Lies* and *Toxic Oil*. Find out more at sweetpoison.com.au.

PRAISE FOR *SWEET POISON*

'An eye-opening read on the health implications of too much sugar in our diet.' GOOD HEALTH & MEDICINE

'What's impressive about *Sweet Poison* is that Gillespie turns complex research on what happens to food inside our body and its relation to weight gain into a good read.' SYDNEY MORNING HERALD

'Comprehensive, thought-provoking and highly readable.' THE AGE

'David Gillespie's groundbreaking book on the dangers of a high sugar intake could well revolutionise the way you diet.' A CURRENT AFFAIR

'*Sweet Poison* is a worthy and impassioned effort by an Australian dad to share his surprising discoveries with struggling dieters and provoke further debate about the obesity epidemic.'
AUSTRALIAN BOOKSELLER & PUBLISHER

'I believe that *Sweet Poison* is one of the most influential books I have ever read. My weight is down (17kg in 10 weeks) and, even better, my blood sugar is down from 8.4 to 5.6.' MALCOLM, VICTORIA

'I've lost 11 kg without being on a diet. It's good to know this book is non-fiction.' STEVE IRONS MP, MEMBER OF THE PARLIAMENTARY INQUIRY INTO OBESITY

THE
SWEET POISON
QUIT PLAN

HOW TO KICK THE SUGAR HABIT
AND LOSE WEIGHT

DAVID GILLESPIE

VIKING
an imprint of
PENGUIN BOOKS

For Lizzie, Anthony, James, Gwendolen,
Adam, Elizabeth and Finlayson.

VIKING

Published by the Penguin Group
Penguin Group (Australia)
707 Collins Street, Melbourne, Victoria 3008, Australia
(a division of Pearson Australia Group Pty Ltd)
Penguin Group (USA) Inc.
375 Hudson Street, New York, New York 10014, USA
Penguin Group (Canada)
90 Eglinton Avenue East, Suite 700, Toronto, Canada ON M4P 2Y3
(a division of Pearson Penguin Canada Inc.)
Penguin Books Ltd
80 Strand, London WC2R 0RL, England
Penguin Ireland
25 St Stephen's Green, Dublin 2, Ireland
(a division of Penguin Books Ltd)
Penguin Books India Pvt Ltd
11 Community Centre, Panchsheel Park, New Delhi – 110 017, India
Penguin Group (NZ)
67 Apollo Drive, Rosedale, Auckland 0632, New Zealand
(a division of Pearson New Zealand Ltd)
Penguin Books (South Africa) (Pty) Ltd
Rosebank Office Park, Block D, 181 Jan Smuts Avenue, Parktown North, Johannesburg 2196,
South Africa

Penguin Books Ltd, Registered Offices: 80 Strand, London WC2R 0RL, England

First published by Penguin Group (Australia), 2010

Design by Evi Oetomo © Penguin Group (Australia)
Cover photograph by Rob Palmer
Typeset in 11.5/17 Berkeley by Post Pre-press Group, Brisbane, Queensland
Printed and bound in Australia by Griffin Press

National Library of Australia
Cataloguing-in-Publication data:

Gillespie, David, 1966–
The sweet poison quit plan : how to kick the sugar habit and lose weight / David Gillespie.
9780670074440 (pbk.)
Weight loss.
Sugar – Health aspects.
Food – Sugar content.

613.28332

penguin.com.au

Contents

Introduction

Sugar makes you fat. It is converted directly to fat by your liver and it destroys your appetite control so that you want to eat more of everything. The more sugar you eat, the fatter you will be. If you stop eating sugar, you will stop gaining weight. Even better, you will start to lose weight dramatically. You will still eat as much as you want of anything you want as long as it doesn't contain sugar. And you won't feel deprived in any way. In fact, you won't feel like you're dieting at all – because you aren't.

I lost 40 kg by simply eliminating sugar from my life. Five years later, the weight is still gone. I didn't do that with a diet (no sane person could). All I did was eliminate the substance that was making me fat and sick: sugar. There's just one little catch (you knew there had to be one, didn't you?). Sugar is as addictive as nicotine, so breaking its grip requires some techniques.

This book sets out a five-step plan for breaking your sugar addiction. None of it is painful or difficult. As long as you follow the rules, before you know it you will have broken your addiction and be on your way to a permanently slimmer and healthier you.

I don't remember my first taste of sugar and neither do you. Perhaps it was in your first feeder cup of diluted apple juice. Sugar is the only highly addictive drug that we feed to babies. By the time any of us are conscious of sugar, we are already well and truly addicted. Our brains have been hard-wired to seek out sugar as surely as the cocaine addict is wired to seek out stuff to sniff.

We don't think of sugar as an addictive drug. We don't have to meet chaps with questionable personal hygiene on street corners to acquire it. There are no warning labels on products containing it. And our health authorities even recommend that we consume it (in moderation, of course). But research tells us that sugar is highly addictive. Not in a smashed-out-of-your-brain, high-as-a-kite kind of way, but in a more subtle, deceiving, I-can-give-up-anytime-I-want kind of way – a bit like nicotine.

Most smokers think they can give up their nicotine addiction easily. That is, until they try to do it. Then they discover there is nothing easy about giving up. But compared to someone addicted to sugar, a smoker has it very easy indeed.

A smoker is addicted to nicotine. Nicotine is found in cigarettes, cigars, tobacco and insecticide. It's not the kind of thing you're likely to come across by accident. Anyone consuming it is doing so very much on purpose. If you decide that you no longer wish to be addicted to nicotine, there is a very short list of things you should do:

1. Do not put cigarette in mouth.
2. If cigarette is discovered in mouth, do not light.
3. Do not drink insecticide.

However, imagine how hard it would be to break an addiction to nicotine if it were in everything you ate and drank – like sugar. Unlike smoking, eating is not optional.

This book is about how to break your addiction to sugar. My first book, *Sweet Poison: Why sugar makes us fat*, is all about the science of exactly how bad sugar is for us. In it I document my personal journey from ignorant fat guy to well-researched healthy guy. I'm not a biochemist or a doctor. In fact, I have no medical training at all. I was simply a very overweight lawyer with a desperate need to know why I could never lose weight no matter how hard I tried.

I had to train myself to read medical journals, to understand what they were saying, and to recognise reputable research from unproven statements. I used my legal training to gather the evidence for and against the theory that sugar was the cause of many (if not most) of the chronic diseases we face today – including my obesity.

I took notes so I could remember how it all worked and those notes turned into a book for people who want to know why sugar is killing them. *Sweet Poison* is also a case study (of one). It not only documents what the science says, but it tells the story of how I used my new knowledge to change my life. I've summarised much of what I found in some of the first chapters of this book.

Sweet Poison doesn't, however, talk about the science of addiction. This is an area of medical science that has expanded significantly in the last few years. The main reason for this is that we are beginning to gain a much clearer understanding of the mechanics of the way our brain does its thing. And along with that understanding comes some very clear ideas about how to mess up these mechanics. I'll be talking about some of the recent studies on addiction as we get into the book.

Once I've convinced you that sugar will make you fat, give you diabetes, clog your arteries and give you Alzheimer's disease (to name just a few of its delights), I will show you exactly how to break your addiction to sugar. Breaking this addiction will not require willpower. And it will not require deprivation. It will, however, require rules that you will need to stick to. Once you break the addiction, you won't need the rules any more. Most people do not feel deprived of cocaine, nor do they have to exercise willpower to avoid purchasing it. This is because most people are not addicted to cocaine. Similarly, you won't need to exercise willpower around sugar or feel deprived when you don't have it once you break the addiction.

> It makes such a difference not having to say 'I am trying a new diet' again and again and yet again. I am sure my friends see me as 'the boy who cried wolf' (or should that be 'the girl who tried diet'?).
>
> I have been sugar-aware for about 10 days, and have lost 2.5 kg – fantastic! And it's so easy. I am walking 'cos I enjoy it and have found a very low or sugar-free version of most things I like. Except chocolate – there was some at work yesterday and, oddly enough, I wasn't even interested.
>
> **Bushturkey***

*The case studies in this book are direct quotes from posts to the free Sweet Poison Forum located at: http://sweetpoison.myfreeforum.org/index.php

Because you're clearly highly intelligent (well, you bought this book, didn't you?), you may already have noticed my first rule in action: I never refer to what you are about to undertake as 'giving up sugar'. 'Giving up' implies deprivation. If you think about this process as depriving yourself of sugar, you will never break the addiction. Having the right attitude is critically important to successfully breaking this (or any) addiction, and the right attitude starts with how you describe what you're doing. You are not giving up sugar; you are breaking a sugar addiction. Start the process now by telling people that this is what you are doing. Go on!

Most diet books give you lots of complicated rules and procedures to follow. *You may eat only an organic grape picked by a gorilla from the north-eastern side of Mt Kilimanjaro between 2.32 p.m. and 3.17 p.m. on a Tuesday in August. It must be eaten whilst balancing on one foot. And you may only eat it in combination with lettuce on Fridays before midday.* But along with all the complexity comes a very basic set of presumptions about how the body works. *Fat makes you fat. Exercise makes you thin. Your liver needs to be detoxified (with lemons?).*

This book is exactly the opposite. The rules are simple and broad. *Eat anything you like as long as it doesn't taste sweet. Eat it whenever you like and eat as much as you like, just stop when you feel full.* Simple. But the reasons for these rules are based on detailed and thorough analysis of exactly how our body deals with food: what hormones are involved and what the cascade of disease effects are. In other words, this is not a diet book with simple presumptions and complex rules; it is an anti-diet book with detailed evidence but simple rules.

In law, we refer to 'bright-line rules'. These occur when, given some objective facts, the outcome is known and predictable every single time, no matter what else is happening. Bright-line rules are to be distinguished from the more touchy-feely case-by-case (or discretionary) rules, in which there is room for interpretation. You experience bright-line rules every day. For example, the law says that if you exceed the speed limit, you have committed an offence. There are no special circumstances to take into account. All the enforcer needs to know is the speed limit and your speed.

An example of a rule that is not bright-line is the one you will confront if you exhaust the points on your driving licence. You will be asked to explain why your licence shouldn't be taken away. You may have very good reasons for needing to retain it and you might be allowed to, with certain conditions. The allowable reasons and the possible conditions will be considered on a case-by-case basis.

Nutritionists are not good at bright-line rules. 'Eat sugar in moderation' is not a bright-line rule because everybody's definition of 'moderation' is different. But you can't have squishy rules when you are breaking an addiction, so you will find only bright-line rules in these pages. These rules will end your sugar addiction, and keep you away from the stuff forever.

In **Re-stocking** (page 96), I guide you through the sugar-infused minefield known as the local supermarket. The **Meal Planner** (page 127) gives you a basic plan for eating without sugar. And once you're 'on the wagon', you can use the **Recipes** (page 191), which include some magnificent treats (like ice-cream and chocolate cake) that you might have thought were simply not possible without sugar. Most importantly, throughout the book you will find the rules you will need (see page 168 for a summary) to get through the withdrawal period and live in a society where almost everybody else is addicted.

By the time you get to the end of this book, you will know how to give up sugar forever. Once you implement the bright-line rules, you will never need sugar in your life again, and you will do it all without exercising even the smallest modicum of willpower.

1. SWEET POISON

Sugar makes you fat. There's no doubt about it. There's not a single research paper done in the last 15 years which would dispute that basic point. And there are over 3000 that will confirm it. But, for reasons which I explore in *Sweet Poison* and take further on my blog (www.raisin-hell.com), you will struggle to find the single bright-line rule that matters most written anywhere. Here it is:

Don't eat sugar.

Even if you can't remember any of the other rules, remember this 'super rule'. It should be printed in bold type in every nutrition guideline. Instead, the message that is given – 'Everything in moderation' – is both vague (your definition of 'moderation' is likely to be different from mine) and misleading (it suggests that there is a safe level of consumption).

Sugar and nutrition – A brief history

In 1810, sugar was considerably rarer than hen's teeth. There was a good reason for this: it was outrageously expensive. We hadn't yet figured out any commercially viable way of turning sugar cane into convenient pretty white crystals. The available methods were intensely manual and not particularly reliable, hence the cost. If you wanted something sweet to eat, it was no good popping down to the corner store. You could grow a nice fruit tree and wait until it was in season or, if you were really adventurous, you could round up some bees and convince them it would be a good idea to give you their honey. That was it – sweetening options 1 and 2. Needless to say, sweet treats were rather limited on the typical dinner table.

By 1910, sugar-based foods were starting to sneak into our diets. In England, Cadbury had just started selling its Dairy Milk Chocolate bar, the first-ever packaged chocolate product. (Until then, Cadbury had made its living selling drinking cocoa.) In the United States, Coca-Cola and Pepsi-Cola were still garage operations run

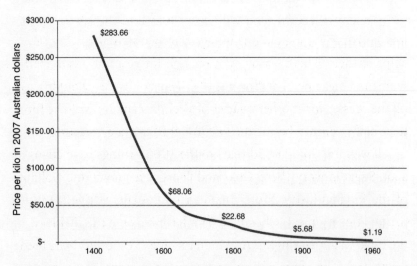

Figure 1.1: English retail price of sugar 1400–1960. Prior to 1800, sugar was priced and used like a condiment.

out of sheds behind the pharmacies of their inventors, but they were growing fast. The total sales of both drinks amounted to a teaspoon of cola for every man, woman and child in the US per year. It would be 14 years before you'd be able to buy breakfast cereal in Australia, and the only place you'd be tasting fruit juice that you hadn't squeezed yourself was in church on Communion Sunday. In fact, it would be another 40 years before you'd be able to buy canned orange juice in Australia. Freshly squeezed juice has a tendency to go off very quickly if it's not refrigerated, and while refrigerators had been invented well before World War II, the costs were prohibitive. It wasn't until mass-market manufacturing of fridges became possible after the war that they came within reach of the average US household.

In 1910, there weren't many overweight people in the US (the only reliable source of such data from this early stage). Four out of every five people were downright skinny by today's standards. There was no such thing as heart disease. (Well, there probably was, but it affected so few people that it was not regularly diagnosed.) The medical specialty of cardiology would not even be necessary for another 25 years. No one was getting rich selling gym memberships or diets. There wasn't even enough interest in diets to start a women's magazine. The first copy of *Women's Weekly* wouldn't roll off the presses for another quarter of a century and it would be more than half a century before the first Weight Watchers' meeting.

If we jump forward 50 years to the 1960s, things have changed a lot. Sugar is everywhere. Coke and Pepsi have grown into Goliaths of the food industry. Fruit juice can be bought, refrigerated and drunk at every meal. Chocolate bars have become the lifeblood of the huge Cadbury empire. And imitators like Nestlé and Mars aren't far behind. The range of breakfast cereals has grown from the corn flakes offered in the 1920s to thousands of high-sugar concoctions.

Breakfast cereal sales are doubling every nine years. And that isn't the only thing doubling. The number of overweight people in the population has doubled in just five decades.

In the 1960s, heart disease was endemic; it caused two out of every three premature deaths in the US. A health disaster was clearly in progress, so cardiologists were trained at a rate never seen before for any profession. Medical schools were endowed with fortunes. Drug companies launched massive research programs, with government money helping to grease the wheels.

The search for answers started with the invention of a new profession: human nutrition. Employees in this field were asked to figure out why we were all suddenly dying from heart disease. It didn't take them long to discover that heart disease is caused by a build-up of fat (cholesterol) in the arteries, and that eating fatty foods causes this build-up. They noticed that fat people didn't seem to exercise much, so they came to the conclusion that the failure to exercise was the cause of obesity. They didn't bother too much with the equally viable alternative observation that fat people didn't exercise *because* they were fat.

Since at least the 1940s, doctors had supported the proposition that if you exercise more, you will eat more. Most of the medical profession suggested (perhaps logically) that bed rest was more likely than exercise to help with obesity, since exercise only prompts consumption. One leading medical textbook at the time (*Obesity and Leanness* by Hugo R. Rony, 1940) observed that lumberjacks ate twice as much as tailors and concluded that 'vigorous muscle exercise usually results in immediate demand for a large meal'. So, it shouldn't come as much of surprise that study after study since then has failed to establish any direct link between weight loss and exercise.

But the logic of this and the opposition of the medical profession didn't stop the nutritionists. The biggest supporter of the exercise-makes-you-thin message was influential French-American nutritionist, Jean Mayer. Aided and abetted by the newly created sports shoe and sports clothing industries, the message gained momentum to the point where, today, we are faced with incessant state-sponsored cajoling towards exercise as a solution to our obesity problem.

The other cause of obesity (according to the human nutritionists) boiled down to the insightful idea that 'you are what you eat'. It was obvious to even the dullest nutritionist that if you eat fat, you will become fat. At the urging of these newly minted experts, we all went on low-fat diets and took up the brand new sport of jogging. Never before in human history had it been necessary to run for a purpose other than to catch food or get away from danger; never before had shoes been designed specifically for running; and never had venues for 'working out' been needed for anyone except prisoners. Yet sports clothing and fitness empires were created in the blink of an eye. Food manufacturers made low-fat everything. We ate even more breakfast cereals and drank more juice and soft drink because none of these things had the devil (i.e. fat) inside. Even the doctors did their bit: they used all that extra money to figure out ways of replacing bits of clogged-up artery with bits cut from our legs. As a result of all this, the death rate from heart disease has now halved to 'only' one in three deaths. Unfortunately, obesity levels have not decreased.

In the 50 years since we invented the profession of human nutrition and started listening to what the experts told us, the percentage of overweight people has doubled again. Now the skinny guy is the odd man out. The numbers shown in Figure 1.2 are for the US. They have a head start on us, but we are not far behind. In the last decade alone, the number of overweight and obese Australians jumped from 41.1 per cent in 1998 to 59.3 per cent of the adult population.

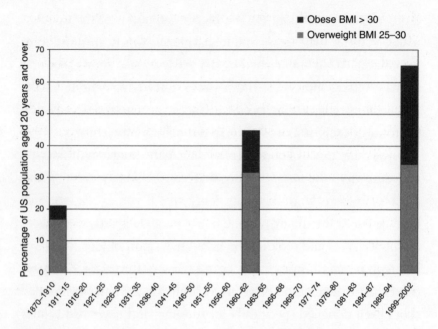

Figure 1.2: Overweight and obese in the US adult population

Now, type 2 diabetes, which was not even recognised as a disease in its own right prior to 1965, is taking over as the new killer. And our health systems are collapsing under the weight of treating the complications of what are believed to be weight-related diseases that simply did not exist five decades ago. When these stark realities are presented to politicians, there is the usual wagging of the fingers at us, the slothful masses. Clearly we have not been listening to the expert advice: we need to eat less fat and exercise more. But the numbers tell a different story.

Fat consumption has been steadily declining for 20 years. And the health equipment, gym and weight-loss industries have all gone from being worth zero to billions of dollars in just 30 years. Forget about the internet boom; the boom in the 'health' industry has been sustained like nothing in our economic history.

According to the Australian Sports Commission, in 2008 more

than 70 per cent of us exercised at least once a week and almost 50 per cent participated in sport three or more times a week. However, these numbers should be treated with caution because they are based on self-completed survey forms. (We all tend to exercise more when filling out surveys!) Money may be a more reliable indicator. According to the Australian Bureau of Statistics, between 1998 and 2004, we spent almost 20 per cent more on physical activity, including a whopping 92 per cent increase in the number of gym memberships we purchased.

Even in the US, where all kinds of unwelcome records are being set for obesity, the figures don't match the message that we're not exercising. According to the National Federation of State High School Associations, the number of students participating in high-school athletics has just increased for the nineteenth consecutive year. And it's not just the kids. Their parents have been spending up big on sports gear. Sporting apparel sales are up 35 per cent since 2000 and sports shoe sales are up 44 per cent. Sports equipment sales more than doubled between 1990 and 2008 (from $30 billion to almost $70 billion).

But perhaps we are just enrolling in gyms and filling our cupboards with gym equipment and gear to make us look like we exercise (believe me, it happens). A better test would be a fitness activity that we pay for only when it is really used. Personal training is a very high-growth industry in the US and Australia. In 1999, there were 127 310 personal trainers in the US. That figure almost doubled, to 219 990, in 2007. Australian data shows a similar trend. In the 2006 census, 13 800 people said they were employed as fitness instructors, up from 7669 in the 1996 census.

The numbers don't lie. Most of us are exercising much more than we used to, but we're still getting fatter at an alarming rate. And this isn't just some phenomenon of the former colonies. More people in

Britain do the recommended amount of exercise (at least 30 minutes of moderate-intensity activity at least five times a week) than did 12 years ago. And over the last five years, the amount spent on gyms has grown by 50 per cent, to more than £1.25 billion every year.

I know how hard it is. I have tried everything from walking for miles to starving myself . . .

The body is an amazing thing; it likes to take care of itself. So when I exercised more, my body would get hungrier to fuel my extra exercise. And when I cut out certain foods, my metabolism would slow down because my body needs all the food groups to make my metabolism work efficiently. And when I lowered the amount of food I ate, my body would store all it could as fat because it thought I was starving and it needed to build up my fat stores.

So, you see, I have tried everything to lose weight. Now I can say I have lost 10 kg in the last six months, eating more than I have ever eaten before of all the five food groups. I am not on a diet and will never go on one for the rest of my life. I intend to eat all the lovely food that I like.

I'm feeling healthier than I have for at least 30 years, and it costs me nothing!

This may sound like an ad, but it is all the things I have learned since I started gaining weight for no reason – well, I thought for no reason. The culprit is innocent sugar.

Marita

Sugar purveyors (like Cadbury, Coke, Pepsi, Mars and Nestlé) that barely existed a century ago now sit astride billions of dollars in annual revenue. Breakfast cereal makers reap hundreds of millions in profits and fully half of the US corn crop gets turned into sugar to put into soft drinks. Is there an elephant in the room? 'Big Sugar' (far stronger now than Big Tobacco ever was) assures us there isn't, and diverts our attention with talk of 'everything in moderation'. But the elephant is getting hard to ignore. For decades, researchers unable to prove that feeding rats fat makes them fat have been proving that feeding them sugar not only makes them fat but gives them heart disease, type 2 diabetes, fatty liver disease and testicular atrophy.

These studies have been dismissed or swept under the carpet by Big Sugar (ably assisted by nutritionists). Everyone knows that if you give a rat a big enough dose of anything, you can make it sick – or dead. But then someone just as powerful as Big Sugar started to look for a different answer. The drug companies who had got rich from cholesterol-lowering drugs started looking for a 'cure' for obesity and type 2 diabetes.

When you have to make a drug that works, it's not good enough to guess that fat causes fatness or diabetes, and it's not good enough to guess that exercise has anything to do with changing it. Biochemists (on drug company payrolls) started looking at what we actually did with our food rather than making 'educated' guesses, as the nutritionists had been doing. Money tends to focus the attention of researchers, and a lot of progress was made during the nineties and naughties. Important new appetite-related hormones were discovered and what emerged from two decades of work was a scientific consensus as to how we digest food and how our appetite control system works.

Research found that we are designed for equilibrium. Like all other animals, we won't get fat unless our appetite control system is broken in some way. This was a key discovery. It is simply not plausible to suggest that over 70 per cent of the population has suddenly lost the ability to eat properly, so something must have broken our appetite control during the last 150 years.

Primary food groups

Our food can be divided into three primary groups:

Carbohydrates are edible plant and seed material such as fruits, vegetables, grains and sugars. Since we're not that close to the land these days, you'll recognise them as the more highly processed foods like bread, biscuits and breakfast cereals. Carbohydrates are made when plants convert energy (sunlight) into stored sugars.

Proteins are organic compounds found mostly in meat. They are created by animals when they eat carbohydrates. Animals (including us) use carbohydrates for energy and for growing proteins in the form (largely) of muscle. Omnivores like us can shortcut the plant-to-muscle process by eating another animal and stealing its proteins.

Fats are energy storage systems used by plants (oils) and animals (fats). Fats don't contain water, so they can be used to store almost twice as much energy as an equivalent amount of carbohydrate or protein. Fats are a great shortcut to energy for an animal that hasn't eaten for a while; just suck down some fat and you have instant energy.

When the guesswork stopped and the research started, the hormones told the story. When we eat fat and protein, a hormone is released by our gut that tells us to stop eating when we've had enough. And when we eat carbohydrates, a different hormone is released by our pancreas that does the same thing.

Except, there is one carbohydrate that doesn't trip the appetite control switch: fructose. Fructose is one-half of sugar (see box, page 17). Everything that contains sugar contains fructose. Our bodies do not detect fructose as a food and our livers convert it immediately to fat. Before you even finish your glass of apple juice, the fructose in the first mouthful will be circulating in your bloodstream as fat.

The important sugars

Carbohydrates are broken down into simple sugars by our digestive system. There are only three important simple sugars: glucose, fructose and galactose. All of the other sugars you are likely to encounter in daily life, including sucrose, are simply combinations of these three.

Glucose is by far the most plentiful of the simple sugars. Pretty much every food (except meat) contains significant quantities of glucose. Even meat (protein) is eventually converted to glucose by our digestive system. Glucose is our primary fuel – no glucose means no us.

Galactose is present in our environment in only very small quantities and is found mainly in dairy products in the form of lactose (where it is joined to a glucose molecule).

Fructose is also relatively rare in nature. It is found primarily in ripe fruits, which is why it is sometimes call 'fruit sugar'. It is usually found together with glucose and it is what makes food taste sweet. As well as fruit, it is naturally present in honey (40%), maple syrup (35%) and agave syrup (90%).

Sucrose (sugar) is what we think of when someone says table sugar. It is composed of one-half glucose and one-half fructose. Brown sugar, caster sugar, raw sugar and low GI sugar are all sucrose.

Immediate conversion to circulating fat would not be such a big deal if we didn't eat much fructose. But we now eat an awful lot. In 1810, the average Australian's primary source of fructose was the occasional piece of ripe fruit. And you could only get the fruit where it grew; there were no refrigerated aircraft flying bananas from Brazil to Australia in the middle of winter. The fruit plus a bit of honey amounted to, at most, 1 kg of fructose per person per year.

By the sixties, when two out of every three premature deaths were being caused by heart disease, Americans were consuming 24 kg of fructose per person per year. The breakfast cereals, fruit juices and soft drinks introduced immediately after World War II were the primary reason for the enormous acceleration in sugar consumption.

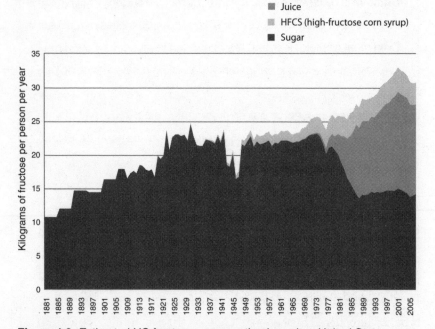

Figure 1.3: Estimated US fructose consumption based on United States Department of Agriculture data. Honey and syrups add about 1 kg per year to these figures. Australia does not have HFCS, but total sugar consumption (excluding juice) is about 50 kg per year (25 kg per year of fructose). The explosive growth in retail juice bars in Australia during the last five years has resulted in significant growth in Australian juice consumption.

By the year 2000, the American population had pushed that up to 33 kg of fructose per person per year (that's about a kilogram of fructose per person every 10 days). By then, almost 15 per cent of the average person's daily calorie intake was coming from fructose. In the last decade, consumption has edged back down to 30 kg per person per year, thanks largely to the introduction of a huge number of high-intensity sweeteners in drink. However, the most recent data shows fructose consumption starting to rise again. And, unfortunately, that is nowhere near the worst of it. The researchers also found that if you put that much fat in your arteries, you mess up your appetite control system for those foods that do trigger it.

If there is too much fat in our bloodstream, hormones like insulin, CCK and leptin (which tell us when to stop eating – see box, page 20) no longer work as well as they should. It's as if our appetite control system is stuck at half-off. The hormonal signals telling us to stop eating cannot cut through the noise from all the fat. And since we're not told to stop, we keep eating. So not only is fructose undetected and turned to fat, it actually increases the amount of other food we eat. This is likely the reason why, in the three decades between 1970 and 2000, the average American increased their daily calorie intake by 25 per cent. In the same period, they increased their (sugar-sweetened) soft drink and juice intake by 63 per cent (see Figure 1.4).

As we keep eating, the carbohydrates keep being converted to blood sugar. Blood sugar keeps rising and we eventually cannot produce enough insulin to remove the sugar from our bloodstream. Doctors describe this state as insulin-resistance, the first stage of type 2 diabetes. Thirteen per cent of the US adult population is now suffering from type 2 diabetes. The equivalent number in 1965 was close to zero. When you add in those with insulin-resistance (knocking on the door of the disease), the number soars to 40 per cent of the population.

A crash course in hormones

There are four critical hormones in our appetite control system:

CCK (cholecystokinin) is released when we eat fat and protein. The more of it we eat, the more CCK is released. An accumulation of CCK in our bloodstream signals to our appetite control system that we have had enough to eat.

Insulin is released by our pancreas. The pancreas monitors the level of glucose in our bloodstream. Glucose is the end product of eating all carbohydrates except fructose. As an appetite control signal, insulin works in exactly the same way as CCK.

Leptin is a hormone released by fat cells in our body. The more fat cells we have, the more leptin is released. So, if everything is working properly, leptin acts as a kind of long-term fuel gauge for our appetite control system. It works as an appetite suppressant in the same way that CCK and insulin do. It ensures that our default appetite state is 'not hungry'.

Ghrelin is a hormone released by our stomach lining. It forces our intestine to contract (causing that bubbling, gurgling feeling you get when you're hungry) and reverses the effects of leptin. It acts as a temporary 'on' switch for our appetite control system, i.e. it stimulates our hunger.

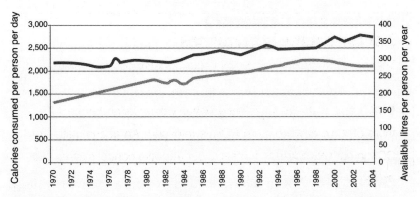

Figure 1.4: Calories consumed (black) versus sugar-sweetened soft drink and juice available (grey), 1970–2004

Fructose vs glucose

A recent study at the University of California persuaded 32 over-weight and obese people to try a 10-week diet which was either 25 per cent fructose or 25 per cent glucose. Both the glucose and the fructose were in addition to what the people normally ate, so you'd expect them all to put on weight – that's a lot of extra sugar every day. They all put on weight, as expected, but the people on the fructose diet ended up with increased (1.5 kg) abdominal fat whereas the people on the glucose diet did not. Abdominal fat has been shown to be a definitive sign of heart-attack risk, whereas fat stored in other places (such as the arms or legs) is not. The fructose group also had much higher blood triglyceride – that's the circulating fat created by the fructose, which leads to heart disease. Their insulin-resistance (a precursor to type 2 diabetes) was 20 per cent higher.

Persistently high blood sugar is the most immediate effect that fructose consumption has on our bodies. Eventually that translates into obesity and type 2 diabetes. But researchers are digging up even worse news.

Diabetes and dementia

For a long time, researchers have known there is a strong relationship between type 2 diabetes and dementia. Estimates have varied, but you are approximately two to four times as likely to have dementia if you also have diabetes or a history of insulin-resistance. Now, a bunch of Swedish twins are starting to put some real meat on the bones of the diabetes link.

Almost 14 000 twins participated in a recently published study. The twins were part of the Swedish twin registry and were all over the age of 65. Because they had provided health data to the registry throughout their lives, the researchers had excellent information about their health over a long period.

Twins are great for this kind of work because when one becomes ill but the other doesn't, large tracts of potentially irrelevant causes are eliminated. Clearly the twins share the same gene pool and have (usually) been raised in an identical environment. When dementia sets in early, as it is doing increasingly (15 000 Australians under the age of 65 now have dementia), the number of possible causes is narrowed further.

The study proved beyond any doubt that diabetes is associated with dementia. Even more interestingly, it concluded that the longer you have had diabetes (or insulin-resistance), the more likely you are to develop dementia. In a somewhat depressing footnote, the researchers suggest their estimate (that you are 125 per cent more likely to become demented if you are diabetic) is probably a bit conservative because so many diabetics die before they are old enough to notice they are losing their grip.

Research published a month after the twin study took the issue further and established a direct link between consuming sugar and 'impaired cognitive function'. Almost 3000 people suffering from type 2 diabetes and aged 55 years and older took part. They were subjected to a battery of tests (part of a standardised set used for detecting early signs of dementia) designed to measure things such as how fast they performed calculations, how well they multitasked, and the accuracy of their memory.

The researchers then compared the results of the tests to measures of each person's average blood sugar reading over time. They found that there was a significant correlation between a person's score on the tests and their blood sugar level. The higher the blood sugar level, the lower their score on all the tests. The researchers noted that a one per cent rise in blood sugar takes you two whole years closer to dementia.

High blood sugar (and ultimately type 2 diabetes) is definitively caused by over-consumption of sugar. But what this latest research tells us is that diabetes is not the end of the story (as if it weren't enough). Lifelong sugar consumption is making us demented – literally.

Effects of fructose

Fructose affects a number of different systems in our bodies in many complex ways. Here is a list of the effects (so far) that researchers have attributed to fructose:

Mineral depletion Collagen and elastin are the building blocks of all our major organs. Fructose seems to interfere with the body's copper metabolism to such an extent that collagen and elastin cannot form properly during growth. Problems in their formation and cross-linking result in impaired muscle growth (in young animals) and problems with vein and artery wall formation (leading to conditions such as varicose veins). Long-term fructose consumption also appears to have a similar effect on skin collagen, leading to premature aging of the skin. Fructose also inhibits the absorption of iodine, which can lead to problems such as an enlarged thyroid gland as well as cretinism (stunted mental and physical growth) in unborn children.

Blood triglyceride elevation When consumed, fructose is immediately converted to circulating fatty acids (triglycerides). This results in a blunting of our appetite control system by rendering us resistant to signals from insulin and leptin (the hormones which tell us when we've had enough to eat). It also leads to type 2 diabetes and a permanently elevated blood sugar level. Consistently high blood sugar provides a perfect environment for cancer growth and is associated strongly with depression, anxiety, polycystic ovary syndrome and dementia. Fructose also causes sustained increases in LDL (low-density lipoprotein) cholesterol levels, leading to increased risk of heart disease and stroke.

Cortisol elevation Fructose produces a spike in cortisol in our bloodstream. Cortisol is a stress hormone and usually only spikes in order to prepare us for a fight (or for running away). It depresses all non-essential functions so the body can focus on the immediate priority of staying alive. One of the non-essential functions it depresses is the immune system, making us more prone to contracting disease. A very recent study out of Stanford University goes further to suggest that a cortisol-induced reduction in immune response leaves breast cancer patients more vulnerable to both their tumours and outside infection.

Uric acid elevation Fructose ingestion results in significant increases in circulating uric acid (a waste product excreted in urine). This leads directly to elevated blood pressure (hypertension), gout (a type of arthritis that occurs when uric acid crystallises in a joint) and kidney disease. It significantly reduces nitric oxide production by the cells that line the interior surfaces of blood vessels. This is bad news for men in particular (and their partners), because we need nitric oxide to maintain erectile function. Viagra works by promoting nitric oxide production; fructose does exactly the opposite.

Central adiposity By consuming fructose, we increase the amount of fat that accumulates around the primary organs, and in particular the liver. Doctors call this 'central adiposity'. Besides making us look less desirable in swimsuits, this leads to something called fatty liver disease and ultimately to cirrhosis of the liver and liver failure.

Similar links between fructose and heart disease, stroke, fatty liver disease (and cirrhosis), cancer, polycystic ovary syndrome, infertility, impotence, depression and anxiety are also starting to appear in well-controlled large-scale trials. Fructose is a perfect storm if the desired outcome is massive rates of chronic (and largely incurable) disease. It's also a perfect storm if you are selling food containing it because we have an insatiable desire for sweetness born of an evolutionary safety mechanism aimed at keeping us away from poisonous foods (which tend to be sour).

Initially, food manufacturers added sugar because they knew we liked it. In 1945, only a quarter of the sugar we ate was already in our food when we bought it. Now, more than three-quarters is already in the food. The reason for this increase is the sugar arms race between producers. The way to sell more product than your competitor is to add more sugar than they do. This is why, for example, in 1978, Kellogg's Special K (in the UK) had 9.6 g of sugar per 100 g; now, this has nearly doubled to 17 g. (The Brits obviously like their Special K a bit sweeter because in Australia it contains 'only' 14.5 g of sugar – so far – and in the US, only 12.9 g.) Australia doesn't monitor food manufacturers as closely as the UK, but I suspect a similar increase would apply here if we were able to compare sugar content in the 1970s to now.

Flying under the fat radar, fructose has crept into almost every food we buy, often under the pretext of making it healthier. We were told to eat more fruit and so we counted dried fruit (70 per cent sugar) and fruit juice (same sugar content as soft drink) as good things – and we fed them to our kids. We were told to eat less fat so we sought out the low-fat products (which needed to be high-sugar to compensate for the lack of fat/flavour). We were told to drink less milk so we switched to zero-fat alternatives like soft drink and apple juice. We were told to avoid high-fat spreads like peanut butter so we switched to 'healthy' honey and fruit conserves. We were told to avoid high-fat breakfasts like bacon and eggs, so we switched to 'healthy' cereals, which were a quarter to half sugar. The miracle is not that we all became overweight or sick; the miracle is that we are not all dead in the face of the incessant fructose doping.

If the only problem with sugar was that it made us fat or sick or both, then it would be easy to fix it on a personal level. We would just need to stop eating anything that contained fructose. Although there is no quick and easy way to tell how much fructose is in most foods, there are ways around this, which I will discuss in chapter 2.

A much more difficult problem facing anyone who decides they no longer want fructose in their life is that it is highly addictive. You don't get to just stop. Whether you know it or not, you are addicted to a substance that is killing you in multiple ways. And just like any other addiction, you will need a plan if you are going to rid yourself of the addictive poison that is fructose.

Diseases linked to fructose consumption (so far)	Indirect links
Weight gain	Sleep apnoea
Type 2 diabetes	Knee failure
Polycystic ovary syndrome	Depressed immune response
Heart disease	Cancer growth in general
Stroke (or aneurism)	Erectile dysfunction
High blood pressure (hypertension)	Pancreatic cancer
Gout	Accelerated aging
Dementia	Impaired muscle development
Depression and anxiety	Cretinism
Fatty liver disease	Varicose veins
Cirrhosis of the liver	
Liver failure	
Acute pancreatitis	
Kidney disease	
Tooth decay	

Surprise! Sugar is addictive

It's the oddest thing. Most of us would acknowledge that sugar is addictive. We joke about it and we even make up words for it (like 'chocoholic'), but I suspect that very few of us really believe we are addicted to sugar. In fact, most of us probably don't believe it's even possible to be addicted to such an innocent thing. Sure, we like it, but if we really had to, we could go without – no problemo. But the reality is that most of us have never tried to give up sugar (at least for more than a few hours) and if we did, we'd have a very different understanding of how addictive it truly is.

Am I addicted to sugar?

1. Do you struggle to walk past a sugary treat without taking 'just one'?
2. Do you have routines around sugar consumption – for example, always having dessert, or needing a piece of chocolate to relax in front of the TV, or treating yourself to a sweet drink or chocolate after a session at the gym?
3. Are there times when you feel as if you cannot go on without a sugar hit?
4. If you are forced to go without sugar for 24 hours, do you develop headaches and mood swings?

If you answered 'yes' to even one of the questions above, you are addicted.

Until recently, very little research had been done on the addictive nature of sugar. It simply hasn't been a priority for addiction researchers because there were apparently more 'serious' targets for research funding such as cigarettes, alcohol and some of the less legal mood alterers. However, now that we are gaining an understanding of exactly how dangerous sugar is, the addiction research dollars have started to flow.

Sugar and dopamine

A Princeton University team has come out with some groundbreaking new work on the exact mechanism of sugar addiction. The researchers, led by Bart Hoebel, presented new evidence demonstrating that sugar can be as addictive to lab rats as heroin or crack cocaine. At the annual meeting of the American College of Neuropsychopharmacology (sounds like fun, doesn't it?)

in Scottsdale, Arizona, Hoebel reported profound behavioural changes in rats that had been trained to become dependent on high doses of sugar. Rats that were denied sugar for a prolonged period after learning to binge worked harder to get it when it was reintroduced to them. They also drank more alcohol than normal after their sugar supply was cut off. (Watch out for that one: going cold turkey on sugar is the best method of breaking the addiction for many people, but you do need to beware of the danger of becoming addicted to something else.)

These rats were being fed a 10 per cent sugar solution, which is what you'd find in a soft drink or fruit juice. And they were becoming dangerously addicted to the point of encouraging other, more dangerous, addictions. The research showed that when hungry rats binge on sugar, a surge of the neurotransmitter dopamine is provoked in their brains. After a month, the structure of their brains adapts to increased dopamine levels, with fewer of a certain type of dopamine receptor than they used to have and more opioid receptors. Opioids are our own little homemade drug supply and include endorphins, the natural peptide associated with

---

Dopamine

Dopamine is a critical component of our fine-motor system as well as our memory, cognition, motivation and reward systems. People with chronically low levels of dopamine lose muscle control and motivation. And the death of dopamine-producing neurons leads to the onset of Parkinson's disease. It's also widely recognised that cocaine and other amphetamine consumption results in the sustained high levels of dopamine that are associated with chemical addiction.

'runner's high'. Rats addicted to cocaine and amphetamines display a similar pattern of dopamine receptor reduction and expansion of opioid receptors. These dopamine and opioid receptors are involved in motivation and reward; they control what our body wants and likes. The result is a significant increase in the drug-seeking behaviour of the rats.

The researchers were also able to induce signs of withdrawal in the lab animals by taking away their sugar supply. The rats' brain levels of dopamine dropped and, as a result, they exhibited anxiety as a sign of withdrawal. Their teeth chattered and, although rats normally like to explore their environment, they were too anxious to leave their enclosures.

Very recent research on the mechanics of addiction suggests that addictive substances do more than stimulate dopamine response; they actually change our brain. These drugs take over our brain's learning function. When we learn or practise something, we strengthen the links between neurons. These strengthened links help us remember and apply knowledge. When researchers repeatedly feed rats cocaine, it appears to hijack this function. Links which reinforce the behaviour of taking the drug are created and thickened, and the rats become hard-wired to seek out that behaviour. This may be the crucial difference between merely enjoying something and being addicted to it. Even worse, the research suggests that as the addiction links in our brain strengthen, we no longer even get the dopamine response – so we keep doing it but can't even pretend it's fun. I guess crack addicts don't really look like they're having much fun, and neither do smokers nor people who've eaten too much sugar.

An addicted person is wired (by the addictive substance) to think that the only way they can feel normal is to have access to the addictive substance. When it's not available, they feel as though something is missing. Their brain reacts by going into mild depression, or even severe depression if the abstinence is prolonged.

Any sugar addict will tell you that sugar makes them feel better. The reality is that before they consume sugar, they are suffering a mild downer caused by the time lapse since the last sugar hit. Taking more sugar simply lifts them back to how an unaddicted person feels all the time. This vicious cycle of mild pleasure followed by mild withdrawal which in turn is relieved by mild pleasure is the simple mechanism of addiction. It is the same no matter which is the poison of choice, from cocaine to sugar. Just because it's sold in supermarkets rather than back alleys doesn't mean sugar is any less addictive or dangerous.

A great little experiment would be to get a group of people and remove their tongues (so you could be certain it wasn't the sweet taste that was stimulating their dopamine response), then give them unlimited access to solutions which were based on either sugar or artificial sweeteners and note whether they developed a preference for either (while measuring their dopamine levels). Recently, some researchers at Duke University in North Carolina did just that. Okay, they chickened out on the tongue-removing thing and they preferred mice over men, but they did manage to obtain a breed of mouse that was genetically unable to taste anything. And guess what? The mice developed an addiction to the sugar solution but not the artificially sweetened solution, even though (to the mice), they both tasted like water.

Researchers are not yet certain exactly how fructose exerts its addictive magic, but they think it may be related to a fact that's been known about fructose since the sixties. They noticed that feeding rats fructose caused a spike in cortisol (see box, pages 23–5). Cortisol is produced by the adrenal gland (the maker of adrenaline). It's often called the stress hormone because it's released by the gland in response to stress. Cortisol gets everything working harder and faster during times of stress (which was particularly handy when a caveman was being chased by a woolly mammoth or a sabre-toothed tiger!). It temporarily increases blood pressure (for faster thinking) and blood sugar (for extra energy) and suppresses the body's immune response (so energy is focused on the more immediate concern of staying alive, rather than the endless hunt for nasty infections). Incidentally, this effect on the immune system may explain a phenomenon that any US general practitioner could confirm. For weeks after Halloween and Easter (the sugariest holidays) each year, their waiting rooms are filled with a deluge of children with colds and flu. Studies done in the seventies showed a definite dip in the ability of white blood cells to fight infection after a dose of fructose (or any sugar containing fructose – they tested sucrose, honey and orange juice as well). The spike in cortisol reduced the effectiveness of the immune system by 50 per cent in the first hour; immunity steadily recovered to be almost back to normal five hours after the fructose was taken. Nothing like this happened with starch (bread) or glucose (which did cause a dip but nowhere near as prolonged).

Cortisol release is normally cyclical. Your body gives you a kick-start in the morning by squirting just a little more than normal into the blood, and tones it down when you are trying to sleep. Pretty much anytime you are about to have a stressful experience (such as confronting a polar bear, taking a maths test or doing a job interview), your body will give you a little squirt of cortisol to get you through. The interesting thing about fructose is that it generates the same cortisol spike but without the stress: fructose actually makes you more alert and focused. But it comes at a price. The cortisol spike (natural and fructose-induced) appears to produce a dopamine spike (which might explain why some people become literally addicted to extreme sports). The difference is that you get a sugar-induced cortisol spike up to 10 times a day (depending on how much sugar you're eating) rather than a natural spike a few times a year (unless you confront a lot more polar bears or do a lot more maths tests than I do). Besides running your immune system permanently at half-mast, this constant fructose infusion creates the building blocks for chemical addiction.

2. HOW TO BREAK THE ADDICTION

There are five steps to breaking your sugar addiction:

1. **Have the right attitude.**
   If you treat this as an exercise in deprivation, you will never succeed. You are ridding yourself of a dangerous toxin and this step shows you how to perform the attitude adjustment you will need to get through the remaining steps.

2. **Eliminate habits associated with eating sugar.**
   Believe it or not, it is possible to enjoy a movie without a litre of soft drink for company. This step shows you how to document your sugar habits and create strategies for keeping the habit, if you need to, but getting rid of the sugar.

3. **Eliminate sugar from your food supply.**
   You'll never break an addiction if your fridge and cupboards are full of the addictive substance. This step shows you what to throw out and what to replace it with.

4. **Withdraw from sugar.**

   Intentionally and purposefully eat the last mouthful of sugar you will ever touch in your life. This step tells you what to expect when you withdraw from sugar and the strategies you can adopt for getting through it.

5. **Re-stock and get ready for the rest of your life.**

   Your home needs to be a sugar-free oasis for you and your family. This step shows you how to do it.

Chemical addiction is something that is still not completely understood by medical researchers. What they do know is that certain stimulants such as amphetamine, caffeine, cocaine, nicotine and (they now know) fructose stimulate the release of dopamine in our brains. Anything you do from which you gain pleasure will stimulate a dopamine response. I enjoy gardening, but I'm not addicted to it. A lack of exposure to garden beds doesn't cause me to become depressed or moody. I don't feel the urge to break into parked cars to steal change so I can buy compost. Gardening stimulates a dopamine release in my brain, but because my dopamine receptors are not suppressed (as they are when affected by a stimulant such as fructose) and my opioid receptors are not increased, the pleasure is passing rather than addictive.

The nature of addiction

Addiction is not about enjoyment. Addiction is about compulsion. Ask any smoker whether their first cigarette was enjoyable and they'll tell you they almost choked. Ask any alcoholic whether their first drink was enjoyable and they'll probably tell you it was repellent.

Addiction is also not a choice we make. People don't choose to keep doing something that will kill them. In fact, most don't want to keep doing it. Most smokers would quit tomorrow if they could. If you've made it this far into the book, you have a clear understanding of why you shouldn't eat sugar. There is no upside and there are downsides by the truckload, from obesity to Alzheimer's and everything in between. But simply telling an addict that ugly things will happen to them has no effect whatsoever. That's why people still buy cigarette packets plastered with photos of diseased lungs and amputated limbs. They know they will eventually pay the price, but right here right now all that matters is the gnawing neuron-driven need to feel good again.

> **Addiction:** uncontrollable, compulsive drug seeking and use, even in the face of negative health and social consequences.
>
> Alan I. Leshner, PhD, Director, United States National Institute of Drug Abuse, National Institutes of Health

Addiction is like wearing tight shoes to work: it hurts a little bit all day long, but it's almost worth doing it just for the fantastic feeling of relief you get when you take them off at the end of the day. Smoking a cigarette delivers exactly the same burst of feeling good after a few hours (or however long it's been since the last drag) of feeling pretty ordinary. Sugar addicts are in the same position except that (for now) we can get our fix without having to see the gangrenous outcome of type 2 diabetes. In fact, food manufacturers are quite happy to ensure that we get our sugar fix in just about everything we eat. We barely have to stagger from one tea break to the next to get our next hit. And, unlike smokers, we can sit right at our desk and get hit after hit in nicely packaged bite-size pieces. It couldn't be easier.

Diets and willpower – doomed to fail

Sugar addiction is such an integral part of our society that we don't even have a word (like 'alcoholic', 'chocoholic' or 'worka-holic') to describe people addicted to sugar. 'Eaters' are addicted to sugar, but you can eat without sugar (something you'll know how to do by the end of this book). So I'm inventing a new word for sugar addicts: 'sugarholics'. Sugarholics today are in the same position that smokers were in the fifties. You used to be able to smoke anytime at work. You didn't have to stop work and stand alone in the middle of a field. You weren't vilified for lighting up in a restaurant. Quite the opposite; if you didn't smoke, you were the weirdo. Today, sugarholics rule the roost. Everybody is addicted from birth. Not eating the birthday cake in the tea-room marks you out as the weirdo. Make no mistake: the task you are about to undertake will not be easy, but it is not an exercise in willpower.

All diets ask us to exercise willpower. We are asked to eat less than we want to, even though our body is screaming at us to have a second helping, or we are asked to spend most of our waking hours exercising like a maniac. Restricting our food intake requires enor-mous willpower for most of us, and the longer we do it, the more willpower we require. Most people don't make it past three months of that kind of will-to-live-sapping treatment.

Researchers have been wondering exactly how long any weight we lose while on a diet stays off. Associate Professor Traci Mann and her team from UCLA decided to review the outcomes of 31 long-term studies of calorie-restricting diets. They found that most people initially lost 5 to 10 per cent of their body weight. But they also found that the majority of people regained all the weight plus a bit more within 12 months. Sustained weight loss was found only in a small minority of participants. So, diets that require willpower just don't work. Even worse than that, they usually ask you to pay for the privilege.

A few years ago, the team at *Forbes* magazine (an influential US magazine for the leaders of the business world) decided to take a good hard look at the numbers. They looked at the 10 most popular diets in the US, calculated how much the special foods required would cost, and averaged out the membership cost (if there was one). They then compared this to the average amount spent by a single person on food ($84 per week at the time). They found that being on a diet cost up to $210 per week (or $126 more than not being on a diet). If you signed up to a gym, add an extra $20 a week (minimum). And if you're feeling really gung-ho, add a personal trainer for an extra $80 a session.

Assume you manage to stick to the plan for 12 months. Over a year, you can expect to spend an additional $6552 on food and $1040 on gym membership for a total cost of $7592 without the personal trainer or $11 752 with the trainer (assuming you train with them for one hour per week). Given that most of us are back to where we started (or worse) within a year after the diet, the eleven and a half grand would probably be better spent on a house deposit.

Just like willpower-based methods of quitting smoking, diets don't work. If they did, there wouldn't be a diet industry. You cannot overcome an addiction by feeling like you are depriving yourself of something. The nature of addiction is that it makes you feel deprived. In between hits of the addictive substance, you endure times of deprivation (or pain, in the tight shoes example). The addictive substance (or when you take the shoes off) is the cure to the deprivation. By definition, addiction makes you feel deprived. If you add to that by consciously feeling deprived, then you are in fact feeding the addiction. A diet that asks you to exercise willpower is doomed to fail because it tells you to feel deprived every minute you do not have access to sugar.

Despite what everybody tells you, if you are a sugarholic, you do not have a personality defect. You are not a glutton. You are not weak-willed. You are chemically addicted to a substance in the food supply called fructose. And until you treat that addiction as the powerful biochemical force that it is, you will never loosen its grip. There are five steps to beating your addiction.

Step 1 – The right attitude

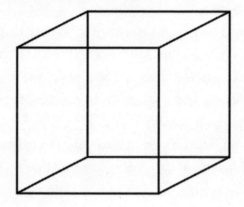

Figure 2.1: Necker Cube

The Necker Cube (named after Swiss crystallographer Louis Albert Necker) is interesting because almost all of us can see it in two different ways. When I first look at it, I see a cube whose front face is bottom left. But if I stare at it long enough, it flips to the top right. You might see it the other way round. Either way, you will be able to see it in both orientations, given enough time.

The Necker Cube is often used to show that our brains are capable of coming to two different conclusions based on exactly the same information. Each conclusion is equally valid and we can switch between each conclusion without the underlying data changing at all. The cube might seem like a party trick, but it's actually an easily understood example of something we do all the time. And our perception of the facts can change our worldview dramatically.

If I told you that you were to be paid $300 000 per annum, your perception of whether that was a good or a bad thing would depend on what everybody else was being paid. If you believe that you are missing out on something that everybody else is getting, then you feel hard done-by. And you will be highly motivated to get a piece of that action. But you have to believe that you are being deprived of a benefit.

What would be your attitude to a substance that, if ingested, would immediately double your waist size as well as your risk of heart disease and type 2 diabetes, and make you a candidate for Alzheimer's disease and a range of cancers? Is there any potential benefit that would make this worthwhile? I'm struggling to think of one. Sugar won't do that to you immediately; you need to remain addicted for 20 years (in most cases). So, does the 20-year delay make it more worthwhile? Does it lower the price? Is there a pleasure you'd be prepared to swap for that, if you get to live 20 years before it happens? Still no from me. How about you?

Like all addictive substances, there is a benefit to having sugar the second and subsequent time. It scratches the addiction itch created the last time/s you consumed it. It relieves the deprivation pressure that builds up from not having the substance. But other than scratching that itch, there is really no significant benefit to be derived from eating it. Think about it. Exactly how is your life improved by having that next piece of chocolate? It will give you that little squirt of good feeling as it hits your tummy – that's the cortisol firing the dopamine response. But other than those few seconds of pleasure, you gain exactly nothing. And every extra piece of choco-late you eat delivers less and less of the little squirt of pleasure until you are chewing just to give your gums exercise (or because there are still chocolates left in front of you).

The hit is the feeling of taking your shoes off at the end of the day. It returns you to normal and that does feel good, but it is very temporary. As soon as you stop taking the addictive substance, the shoes are back on and you feel steadily worse until you get to take them off again. The only people envious of heroin addicts are other heroin addicts. Everyone else can see plainly that the downsides outweigh any small possibility of an upside. The only people envi-ous of sugar addicts are other sugar addicts. Unfortunately, in our society, that's most of us from the age of our first word onwards. Once you are no longer an addict, it's very hard to see any benefit at all.

The sugar hit momentarily returns you to normal; it doesn't lift you to a better place. If sugar wasn't part of your life, you would feel 'better' all the time. You want sugar because it takes you to a better place (for a moment or two), but the very act of taking it pushes you to a worse place until you have it again.

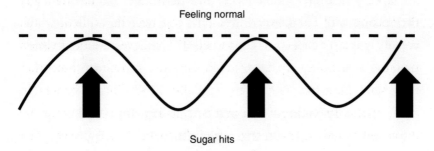

Figure 2.2: A day (or an hour) in the life of a sugarholic – sugar simply returns the sugarholic to normal in between bouts of deprivation

Perform the flip

So, there are lots of downsides to sugar addiction and the only upside is that you feel normal when you have a hit. Do you really have cause to feel deprived? No, but willpower diets demand that you feel deprived. They ask you to 'go without' and to 'give up' a treat. Feeling deprived will simply drive you back into the arms of addiction. The only way to break the addiction is to perform a Necker Cube flip and see the so-called deprivation as a desire not to be poisoned. Or you could consider yourself to be suffering from an intolerance to fructose, and when you consume it you become fat, bloated, lethargic and sick (see Paul's case study, pages 94–5). In that sense, we are all fructose-intolerant, and if thinking about it like that helps you stay away from the addictive toxin in your diet, then it is an important mental tool in your armoury for getting through withdrawal.

If you want to succeed, you mustn't feel you are being deprived of anything. You need to take pity on the poor hopeless addicts who are all around you ingesting poison. You need to view any offering of sugar not as a temptation to be overcome but as an attempt to poison you (perhaps a little extreme, but you get the idea).

So, don't feel deprived. You are not giving up anything. You are simply stopping a dangerous and harmful addiction. It really is that simple to break an addiction. If you have the right attitude, staying sugar-free becomes a lot easier than you could possibly imagine.

Rule 1: Believe you are not being deprived or
Have the right attitude.

> Nothing can stop the man with the right mental attitude from achieving his goal; nothing on earth can help the man with the wrong mental attitude.
>
> Thomas Jefferson (pre-political correctness)

Step 2 – Eliminating habits

Most things in cars are pretty standard. The accelerator is always on the right, the brake on the left. Even in countries where they drive on the 'wrong' side of the road, these things are where they should be. But the one place that car designers have been let off the leash is in the 'let's put the indicator lever somewhere exciting' department.

I drive an old, old car. The engineers very cleverly combined all possible controls into just one lever located on the right of the steering column. So, I'm in the habit of indicating a turn with a flick of my right hand. The trouble is, when I climb into my wife Lizzie's car, the indicator is on the left and I end up putting the windscreen wipers on to turn a corner. This is a habit that's easy to break, but the first few times, my brain runs on autopilot and does the wrong thing. I'm not addicted to using my right hand but at first it might look like an addiction rather than a habit.

Habit vs addiction

Before I became sugar-free, I was in the habit of rewarding myself with a square or two of chocolate in front of the TV at the end of a long (or even a short) day. I was addicted to the sugar in the chocolate. The habit of eating it in front of the TV was not part of the addiction but it did reinforce it. Relaxing in front of the screen is pleasurable – much like gardening is (for some people). But neither of them is addictive in the chemical sense. Habits do, however, reinforce chemical addictions. They grow around the addiction and protect it from your attempts to break it.

A critical step in breaking your sugar addiction is identifying the habits associated with the addiction. For me, watching TV was a means of relaxation, and it still is. But my sugar addiction had infiltrated that pleasurable experience and made it its own. Sugar had become an integral part of the relaxation process. The pleasure I gained from watching TV was directly associated, in my mind, with the dopamine hit I got from the sugar. It's possible to disassociate the two activities but you won't do it by abstaining from both using willpower.

The trouble with addictions is that they frequently attach themselves (like pleasure-sucking parasites) to otherwise pleasurable (but not addictive) experiences and it becomes impossible to distinguish the two. You relax in front of the telly and eat chocolate. The 'relaxing' bit is actually the pleasurable experience but I'll bet the chocolate gets the credit because it delivers the 'just took off the tight shoes' experience. Because the habit and the addiction so tightly reinforce each other, the habit becomes a nasty trigger when you are trying to break the addiction. The time you will most want sugar is when you habitually had it before. You will feel you can't relax in front of the TV without chocolate. Or celebrate Easter without it, either.

Those habits will really test your resolve because of the strong association, and in some cases the strong peer group pressure (at birthday parties, Easter, Christmas etc.) to conform. In many instances, the only rational way to deal with the problem is to avoid the habitual events associated with consuming sugar until you break the addiction. The thing to remember is that you are not giving up pleasurable habits forever. There is nothing intrinsically wrong with the habit, but it is hiding a chemical addiction. Once that addiction is broken, you can safely resume the habit. In some cases, you'll be able to maintain the habit but replace the sugar involved with a sugar-free substitute.

So, if you are in the habit of relaxing in front of the TV with a chocolate at the end of the day, stop watching TV and find some other way to relax in the evening for the next month. Or, in this case you could continue your TV habit but replace the chocolate with nuts, for example.

> We all know breaking a sugar addiction can take up to three or four weeks. It was about four weeks, for me. Now, five months later, my habits and associations have gone. You may be asking, what do you mean?
>
> I know someone who gave up smoking and broke the addiction quite quickly – a matter of two weeks. Although it wasn't until eight months later that he stopped reaching for the smokes in the console of the car whenever he jumped in.
>
> My associations with high-fructose foods have finally gone! For 35 years or even longer (I'm 41), I smothered my food in barbecue sauces and relishes. I couldn't eat anything without them. The biscuits and chocolate were always eaten and none were ever saved for the next day.
>
> Those long-term associations have now gone. I no longer look at the biscuit or confectionery aisle and think, hmmm, I'd like to buy that. Nor when I open the fridge do I think I'll just have one glass of juice or a chocolate biscuit from my flatmate's stash.
>
> **AJ**

You will need to do this (stop the habit or substitute the sugar) for all pleasurable habits associated with sugar consumption.

Believe it or not, you have quite a few, so the first thing to do is to make yourself a list of your sugar-eating habits. The daily habits are the ones you will have to confront first and frequently, so they need to be at the top of the list. Don't get too concerned about the sugar in the food you eat at mealtimes (except dessert) at this stage; that consumption is not habit-based (unless you count staying alive as a nasty habit). Chapter 3 deals with eliminating sugar from your regular food supply. What we are concerned about here is the between-meal snacking habits that involve sugar.

Rule 2: Do not snack on sugar.

My list of habits before I broke the addiction looked like this:

1. Every time I have a cup of tea (which could be five or six times a day), I accompany it with a biscuit (or three).
2. I always have a juice with breakfast.
3. I always look forward to a dessert after dinner.
4. I always eat a few pieces of chocolate in front of the TV at night. On weekends, this might extend to a chocolate-coated ice-cream.
5. If I'm buying a coffee, I get myself a blueberry muffin to go with it.
6. When out shopping, I cannot walk past a vending machine without acquiring a soft drink.
7. When I'm at McDonald's, I always order the 'meal deal' with a soft drink because it's easier (and probably cheaper). And I finish off the meal by visiting the counter again for a soft-serve cone.
8. In the (unusual) event that I do any serious exercise, I reward myself with a chocolate bar or a fizzy drink or both.
9. When I go to the movies, I always get a large soft drink.

10. If I'm not drinking alcohol, I'm drinking something sweet (usually juice or a soft drink) instead.

11. My alcoholic drink of choice (gin and tonic) involves a mixer (tonic) that is high in sugar.

You need to make a list like this for yourself. Be brutally honest. Think about the last few weeks. When did you snack on sugar? What were you doing at the time? Any time you identify a habitual behaviour that also involves eating (or drinking) sugar, put it on the list. Put the book down now and make your list. Don't pick it up again until you're done.

Avoidance strategies

The first step to eliminating habitual sugar consumption is to know that you are doing it. Not in a general 'yeah, I know I shouldn't eat sugar' kind of way, but in a specific 'I know I will eat sugar if do that' kind of way. Now that you have your list (you do have your list, don't you?), you can prepare your avoidance strategies for the withdrawal period. Remember, this will not be permanent. You can go back to your old habits once you break the addiction, because then they will not involve sugar.

My list of avoidance strategies looked like this:

1. Keep a jar of nuts by the kettle and remove the bikkies. That way I can still have a snack when I have a cuppa, but sugar won't be an option.

2. Substitute milk or water for fruit juice with breakfast.

3. Remove all sugar-containing dessert ingredients from the house. Enjoy a non-sugar treat (perhaps some potato crisps) after dinner.

4. Substitute nuts for chocolate for my TV-watching snack.

5. When I buy a coffee, choose a non-sugar accompaniment (like buttered thick toast). If the establishment doesn't offer

a non-sugar option, choose a different coffee purveyor.

6. When I spot a vending machine out shopping, choose a bottled water or a diet drink instead of a full-strength soft drink.

7. At McDonald's, substitute diet soft drink in the 'meal deal' and an apple pie for the after-meal treat.

8. If I exercise, give myself a non food–based reward: shout myself to the movies or drop by the video library on the way home (but see also 4. and 9.).

9. Switch to diet soft drink at the movies.

10. Switch to diet drinks when out or just drink (unflavoured) mineral water.

11. Switch to a diet tonic water in my G&T.

It is very important to write down your list of avoidance strategies. Not so that you can carry them around with you (you might but it probably won't be necessary), but because it forces you to identify your sugar habits and apply your mind to exactly what you will do to avoid the sugar. A strategy of 'I'll cope somehow' will not be good enough. You need to have a plan for exactly what you are going to do to avoid sugar in those situations. If you are stranded at a counter full of muffins with no plan, guess what you'll be having with your coffee! You need to know that your local coffee shop does indeed serve buttered toast. You need to know that the vending machine at the local supermarket has zero-sugar options and if it doesn't then you need to shop elsewhere (or whatever other strategies are appropriate for your list).

I was lucky in that none of my strategies required me to stop the habit altogether. I was in the fortunate position of working from home, so I could control my immediate environment. Many people face a work environment where simply removing the sugar is not an option (unless they wish to win the 'most unpopular at work' award).

When your habit involves eating sugar controlled by others, you will need to stop that habit until you break your addiction. It is not reasonable (or possible) to stop eating a sweet biscuit with your morning cuppa when it is there in front of you and it's the only choice. You have invested years in developing that habit. You will not break it by thinking positive thoughts alone. In that situation, if there is not a non-sugar option available, you need to change the habit to one where you will not be exposed to sugar. Take your own supply of nuts to work and place them next to the biscuits (with appropriate warnings about arm-amputation for trespassers). You will still stray towards the biscuits, but you will have your avoidance list front of mind and you will consciously direct yourself to the nuts instead.

Giving up exercise was a viable option for me because I was only doing it to lose weight (and I wasn't actually doing much, anyway). But for some people, exercise has alternative pleasures. The endorphin rush generated is addictive in itself. The good news is that there is no need to give up exercise if you really do enjoy it. Just make sure that what you drink (and eat) during and after the exercise is sugar-free. Don't reward yourself with a chocolate bar just because you think you've earned it. Change the reward to something without sugar (how about a nice packet of potato crisps?). If you really can't exercise without the sugary reward, then you need to stop exercising for a month or so. It's okay, you'll be able to do it again when you've broken the addiction.

You're probably thinking this doesn't sound much like a way to lose weight. And you'd be right. At this point we are concentrating on breaking an addiction. In substituting nuts for sweet biscuits, you are probably not reducing your overall calorie intake at all. But what you are doing is breaking the connection between pleasurable habits and sugar, which is **Step 2** in becoming sugar-free.

Your list of avoidance strategies may change. No doubt you will have missed some things. Sugar can often be part of a habit without you even realising. It took me a while to add number 11 to my list – it hadn't even occurred to me that tonic water was full of sugar. It didn't taste like it to me at that stage. You will also develop new habits, sometimes as a way of avoiding the old habits. Going to a coffee shop was not on my original list. It got there because I would go out to avoid the biscuit jar. So, be vigilant and make sure your list is accurate. Every time you identify a new situation that encourages you to consume sugar, work out a coping strategy and add it to the list.

Remember that you won't be doing this for the rest of your life. It's only necessary while you are still addicted to sugar. Most people who are no longer addicted to a substance do not need a coping strategy to avoid contact with it. Ask an ex-smoker what he thinks of hanging around people who smoke. Ex-addicts are often the most aggressive avoiders of the substance to which they were addicted. Once your sugar addiction is broken, a triple-layer chocolate cake sitting next to your cuppa will not be the remotest bit tempting. When you break the addiction, you can resume your habits safe in the knowledge that you will not even consider sugar to be part of the pleasure. In fact, you will look back at yourself and wonder what possessed you to shove poison down your throat while having an otherwise enjoyable time.

An important footnote to this section is that it would be very foolish indeed to attempt to break your sugar habit at a time when sugar consumption is almost compulsory. Deciding to start breaking a sugar addiction the day before Christmas or on Easter Sunday is almost a guarantee of failure. Equally, if you know that in the next month you will be attending a large number of social events where you will be required to eat sugar (perhaps your close friends all turn 40 this month), then it might be a good idea to postpone breaking the habit. The withdrawal period is going to be hard enough without choosing to do it at a time when the social pressure to conform will be at its maximum.

Last week, the ambulance volunteer crew that I work with on weekends had their annual Christmas party: There on the table was a real Aussie treacly luscious pineapple upside-down cake. I'd lost 10 kg, so for a bit of Christmas naughtiness, I had two slices of sugary tangy cake with vanilla-flavoured unsweetened cream – lashings of it.

Next day, the five cups of real black coffee that I make and usually enjoy tasted bitter. At night, there I was, climbing the wall for something sweet.

'Re-educating' myself after only two bits of cake was a bloody hassle for over a week. My morning blood measurement was 8, when previously I'd got it down to 4 and 5. I'm down to 6 and 7 now but it has taken more than a week.

Johnny Kesselschmidt

Once you have broken your sugar habit, that pressure will not bother you. You will be able to find things to eat that don't insult your hosts and you won't be making a big deal of it because by then it won't be a big deal to you. It might be difficult to believe, but it is possible to sit in a room full of people eating Easter eggs and not feel the slightest desire to eat one yourself.

However, you're not ready to start breaking the addiction just yet. We still haven't tackled the biggest source of sugar in your diet: the food you eat to stay alive.

Step 3 – Eliminating sugar

If this were a guide to breaking just about any other addiction, we wouldn't need this step. For anything other than sugar, the harmfully addictive substance is obvious and – once you uncouple it from its associated habits – relatively easy to avoid. But the active ingredient in sugar (from an addiction point of view) is fructose and, thanks to the marvels of modern food production, it is now embedded in almost every food item on the supermarket shelf. So, before you even begin to fight your addiction, you've got to pick your way through a minefield of fructose-filled foods.

This step is all about giving you the shopping strategies you need to prevent too much fructose from contaminating your food supply. Let me tell you from the outset that it is impossible to avoid all the fructose in our foods. That's not a bad thing because science now backs up the somewhat intuitive observation that we are adapted to having some fructose in our food, and able to cope with a small amount. Long before we figured out how to add sugar to everything, fructose was present in our food supply. The difference was that it came in its original packaging (fruit) and it was in relatively short supply.

Research has definitively confirmed that we are able to consume the fructose contained in a couple of pieces of fruit per day (that amounts to about 10 g). The only condition is that it must come packaged with fibre (around 5 g per day or more) in order not to cause damage (see Figure 2.5, page 108, for the fibre and fructose content of popular fruits). At these low levels, the fibre will act to mitigate the damage being done by the fructose and there are unlikely to be any long-term effects. However, the average Australian adult male is actually consuming 60–75 g of fructose every day. A fair proportion of this is embedded in what we would regard as our 'normal' food (i.e. not treats). Our task in this step is to identify those sources of fructose in our diet and dramatically reduce them.

You are going to need some shelf space for all your fructose-free food, so the first thing you need to do is throw out all the food in your larder and fridge that is too high in fructose. Let's walk through it category by category. The most obvious and easiest place to start is with sweet biscuits and confectionery.

Sweet biscuits and confectionery

Chocolate of any description must be sent to a happier hunting ground. The same goes for anything you picked up in the confectionery aisle at the local supermarket. I could prepare a list of the confectionery with the lowest sugar content but there really wouldn't be any point; even the best of the best (i.e. the lowest of the low) is way off any acceptable scale. There are, however, alternatives available; I describe these in chapters 3 and 5.

NUTRITION INFORMATION		
Servings per package: 3		
Serving size: 150 g		
	Quantity per serving	Quantity per 100g
Energy	608 kJ	405 kJ
Protein	4.2 g	2.8 g
Fat, total	7.4 g	4.9 g
– Saturated	4.5 g	3.0 g
Carbohydrate, total	18.6 g	12.4 g
– Sugars	18.6 g	12.4 g
Sodium	90 mg	60 mg
Ingredients: Whole milk, concentrated skim milk, sugar, banana (8%), strawberry (6%), grape (4%), peach (2%), pineapple (2%), gelatine, culture, thickener (1442). All quantities above are averages		

Figure 2.3: An NIP for a tub of fruit yoghurt, courtesy of Food Standards Australia New Zealand (FSANZ)

Before we go any further, it's worth saying a thing or two about labels. Since 2003 it has been illegal to sell most manufactured foods in Australia without including a Nutrition Information Panel or NIP. NIPs must list information on energy (kilojoules), protein, total fat, total carbohydrates and sodium (salt). They are also required by law to break out saturated fats and sugars. A sugar is a type of carbohydrate. That's why sugars are listed as a sub-category in the carbohydrate section (see Figure 2.3, page 53). All ingredients must also be listed in decreasing order by weight. So, the first item in the list is the ingredient present in the largest amount. In the tub of yoghurt NIP, whole milk is (reassuringly) the dominant ingredient.

Australian law does not require a food manufacturer to break down the 'Sugars' section on the NIP. So, many ingredients contain significant amounts of sugar but will not be listed as sugars in the ingredients list. For example, all of the following contain sugar (or are converted to sugar once consumed):

Agave syrup	Honey	Maple syrup
Corn syrup	Lactose	Molasses
Dextrose	Malt	Polydextrose
Fructose	Maltose	Sorbitol
Glucose	Maltitol	Sucrose
Golden syrup	Mannitol	

'Sugars' includes all of the items listed above (and more), but not all of them are equally bad for you. All carbohydrates (including all sugars) except fibre and fructose are converted into glucose by your body. Glucose is the body's primary source of energy. Fibre is not normally digested at all; we need it to help mitigate the damage being done by fructose. Fructose is converted into circulating fat, so it is the only sugar you really need to worry about. Let's take another look at that list but this time with the fructose highlighted (*):

*Agave syrup (usually 90% fructose)
*Corn syrup (usually 55% fructose)
Dextrose (another name for glucose)
*Fructose
Glucose
*Golden syrup (usually 40% fructose)
*Honey (usually 40% fructose)
Lactose (converted to galactose and glucose by your body)
Malt (converted to glucose by your body)
Maltose (converted to glucose by your body)
*Maltitol (converted to fructose by your body)
*Mannitol (converted to fructose by your body)
*Maple syrup (up to 40% fructose)
*Molasses (usually 40% fructose)
*Polydextrose (90% dextrose, 10% sorbitol)
*Sorbitol (converted to fructose by your body)
*Sucrose (50% fructose)

I'll talk about some of the sugar substitutes above in a lot more detail in chapter 4. But for now, let's get back to cleaning out the cupboard.

Sweet biscuits are slightly less bad than confectionery. To make your cupboards truly fructose-free, all the sweet ones should accompany the chocolate to the bin. That being said, I've prepared a list of the ten lowest-sugar biscuits available in Australia today. I don't recommend that you keep these on hand while you are in the withdrawal period, but you might want to know for after you break the addiction, even if it is just to have occasionally.

The 10 lowest-sugar sweet biscuits		
1	Arnott's Lattice	12.0%
2	You'll Love Coles Shortbread Finger	15.0%
3	Coles Smart Buy Scotch Finger Woolworths Home Brand Scotch Finger	15.6%
4	Unibic Shortbread Au Chocolat	16.0%
5	Arnott's Farmbake Butter Shortbread	16.5%
6	Arnott's Shredded Wheatmeal	16.7%
7	Unibic Gingerbread Boys & Girls	16.9%
8	Unibic Viennese Shortbread	17.0%
9	Unibic Cinnamon Stars Shortbread Paradise More-ish Macadamia Cottage Cookies	17.1%
10	Aussie Bush Bikkies Lemon Myrtle Bikkie	17.5%

The percentage column tells you how much sugar is in the biscuit. So, if you were to eat 100 g of Arnott's Lattice biscuits, you would consume 12 g of sugar and, in turn, 6 g of fructose. (Fructose is one half of sugar, with the other half being glucose. So for biscuits, where the only sugar is cane sugar, halve the amount of 'Sugars' in the 'Quantity per 100 g' column on the NIP to get the amount of fructose.) A single Arnott's Lattice biscuit weighs in at about 30 g, so a single biscuit will be delivering about 1.8 g (30 per cent of half of 12 g of sugar) of fructose. Five of these biscuits and you have blown your fructose budget for the day (and will have to tape up your mouth because just about everything has some fructose on board).

Just for fun, I've also produced a list of the 10 highest-sugar sweet biscuits available. Needless to say, you will be placing all of these little darlings in the bin immediately.

	The 10 highest-sugar sweet biscuits	
1	**You'll Love Coles** Bite-size Cart Wheels	62.9%
2	**Cadbury** Crunchie Squiggle Tops	61.1%
3	**Weight Watchers** Fruit Slice	56.1%
4	**Cadbury** Chocolate Wafers	54.6%
5	**Arnott's** Spicy Fruit Roll	54.5%
6	**Arnott's** Sultana & Chocolate Snack Right Fruit Slice	52.0%
7	**You'll Love Coles** Chocolate **Arnott's** Nobles **Arnott's** Sultana Snack Right Fruit Slice	51.0%
8	**Arnott's** Marshians **Woolworths Home Brand** Chocolate **Arnott's** Wafer Fingers	50.9%
9	**Arnott's** Full O' Fruit	50.0%
10	**Arnott's** Tee Vee Snacks Wafer Bites	48.6%

I'll bet there's a few there that caught you by surprise. Weight Watchers Fruit Slice, Arnott's Spicy Fruit Roll, Arnott's Sultana Snack Right Fruit Slice and Arnott's Full O' Fruit are all in the list because of their high dried fruit content. In recent years, food manufacturers have consistently marketed dried fruit as equivalent to fresh fruit (in terms of health benefits), but this is simply not so. For example, compare the sugar profiles of raisins and grapes in the table below:

100 g raisins (dried seedless grapes)	100 g grapes (about 20 Thompson Seedless)
Total sugars: **59 g**, consisting of:	Total sugars: **15.4 g**, consisting of:
Sucrose: 0.5 g	Sucrose: 0.1 g
Glucose: 27.5 g	Glucose: 7.2 g
Fructose: 31 g	Fructose: 8.1 g

The average raisin is about 60 per cent sugar and about half of that sugar is fructose (just like cane sugar). So don't be fooled by the 'It's fruit, so it's healthy' message propagated by those who want you to stay addicted to fructose. A fructose molecule doesn't know or care whether it started life as part of a piece of sugar cane or as part of a grape. There are no varietals of sugar molecules; fructose is fructose no matter where it was grown.

Cracker biscuits

In general, cracker biscuits are low in sugar, but when manufacturers start trying to add exotic flavours, it often results in a (sometimes significant) increase in the amount of sugar. In general, look for the plain or unflavoured version of the cracker, avoid anything that says 'chicken flavoured', and stay away from the exotics. Those in the lowest-sugar list can stay in your cupboard.

On average, you'd eat about 60 g of cracker biscuits in a sitting (about four Salada-style crackers or 15 Jatz-style crackers). Very few of these have large amounts of sugar, but remember that whatever you put on the cracker tends to have a significant sugar content.

The 10 lowest-sugar cracker biscuits		
1	**Sakata** Original Rice Crackers	0.0%
2	**Arnott's** Original Watercrackers **Arnott's** Sesame Watercrackers **Arnott's** Cracked Pepper Watercrackers **Arnott's** Wholegrain Watercrackers	0.1%
3	**Sakata** Plain Minis	0.2%
4	**Arnott's** Savoury Shapes **Arnott's** Sesame Wheat	0.3%
5	**Arnott's** Original Saladas	0.4%

6	Arnott's Sao Nabisco Premium 98% Fat Free Nabisco Premium Bran & Sesame Coles You'll Love Coles Rock Salt Vitabites	0.5%
7	Arnott's Corn Cruskits Nabisco Captains Table Water Crackers Nabisco Captains Table Cracked Pepper Water Crackers Nabisco Captains Table Sesame Water Crackers	0.6%
8	Arnott's Poppy & Sesame Saladas	0.8%
9	Arnott's Cheese & Bacon Shapes Arnott's Roasted Garlic & Parmesan Watercrackers Arnott's 97% Fat Free Multigrain Saladas Paradise Veri Deli Soy & Linseed Crackers	0.9%
10	Arnott's Cheds Sakata Cheese Minis	1.0%

Any of the crackers listed in the highest-sugar list should be in the bin – but there's still plenty to choose from that are fine.

The 10 highest-sugar cracker biscuits		
1	Ryvita Fruit Honey & Oats	21.5%
2	Paradise Veri Deli Spring Onion Crackers	13.5%
3	Sakata Sweet Chilli & Coriander Apero	10.7%
4	Griffin's Chicken Snax	10.3%
5	Sakata Honey & Dijon Mustard Apero	10.1%
6	Sakata Tomato Basil & Cream Cheese Apero	9.6%
7	Griffin's Cheese Snax	9.5%
8	Waterthins Pepper & Chives Paradise Veri Deli Sesame & Poppy	9.3%
9	Nabisco Premium Wheat with Honey	8.9%
10	Woolworths Home Brand Plain round cracker	8.6%

Drinks

Sweetened drinks are a fructose expressway to your bloodstream. The average child can down a small (250 ml) glass of apple juice in less time than it took you to read this sentence. By doing that, they are consuming the juice of three large apples (and without the fibre). It would take my kids most of the morning to eat three large apples, but juice is sucked up in an instant. You could drink a large apple juice and eat a full and hearty meal, but try eating the six large apples that produced the juice and see how far you get with the meal. Drinking sugar is the single most efficient way to get it inside you. Truly vast quantities can be consumed without a second thought. A single 600 ml bottle of Coca-Cola (or just about any fizzy drink) will deliver about 66 g of sugar (33 g of fructose), making a bit of a mess of our daily target of no more than 10 g (see **Step 3**, page 52).

It's much easier to tell you which drinks *are* allowed than to specify the rest. The only drinks you should have in your cupboard or fridge are unflavoured water and unflavoured milk. If you prefer your water with bubbles, then by all means have unflavoured mineral water or soda water. It doesn't matter whether the milk is low-fat or regular. (There is some interesting research on low-fat products that suggests you are much better off with the full-fat version, but I'll talk about that in more detail in **Low-fat foods**, page 98.)

If you read the chapter on artificial sweeteners (chapter 4) and are still quite happy to drink diet soft drinks, then you can keep these. When I was going through withdrawal, I desperately needed artificially sweetened drinks. As you can see from my list of habits (page 46), many of my bad sugar habits were associated with soft drinks. I drank them when I went shopping, when I went to the movies, when I ate out and when I drank alcohol – and even when I was out but not drinking alcohol. So, many of my withdrawal coping strategies involved substituting artificially sweetened drinks on each of those occasions. I would not have got through withdrawal without them and if you are as big a user as I was, you probably won't either. The interesting thing is that after withdrawal, you won't be hankering after artificially sweetened drinks. Because you will lose your desire for sweetness, these drinks will seem like strange-tasting substitutes for water. When fizzy drinks lose their addictive kick, there's not much to recommend them, especially if they also taste oddly metallic.

All other juices, soft drinks and flavoured milks must make their way into the rubbish bin. It doesn't matter whether you hand-squeeze the juice or buy it in a bottle; it's still just sugar and water, and it needs to go. Some people object to me describing juice as 'soft drink without the fizz'. They usually cite the nutrients in juices as a reason to keep them in your diet. However, the research does not back up that position. The primary nutrients in most juices are vitamins A and C. But the best that recent large-scale studies on the benefits of supplementing your diet with those nutrients can come up with is that they probably won't cause too much harm. There is no suggestion that supplementing with those vitamins is of any benefit to the average member of western society. And, of course, there is nothing you will get from a juice that you wouldn't also get from the fruit from whence it came. So, if you are utterly convinced that your life will be poorer without the nutrients found in a glass of orange juice, then eat the orange instead. This way, not only will you get the nutrients, you'll also get the fibre.

You may be wondering about soy milks. Soy milks are pri-marily created for people who are lactose-intolerant (lactose is the sugar in cow's milk). Most baby mammals, including humans, are adapted to survive on lactose when they are young, but about 70 per cent (i.e. the majority) of the world's adult human population are lactose-intolerant and cannot digest lactose or use it for energy production. As they reach adulthood, these people lose the ability to manufacture the enzyme that chops lactose into galactose and glucose. People with ancestry in northern Europe, the Middle East and India (the places where people have the longest association with domesticated cattle), are more likely to continue to make the enzyme. These people (including most of the Australian population) are able to continue to drink and eat milk products comfortably into adulthood. For everybody else, the products pass straight through the digestive system, which is why a primary symptom of lactose-intolerance is diarrhoea.

Unfortunately, soy milks must also go. Milk requires sugar if it is to taste anything like milk. Soy milk manufacturers generally use cane sugar instead of lactose. This immediately removes soy milk from the list of acceptable drinks for someone wanting to break a sugar addiction.

How much sugar would you like in your milk?
Here's some popular Australian soy milks with their sugar contents. A small glass (250 ml) contains this much sugar (1 teaspoon of sugar is 4.2 g):
VitaSoy (original): 8.75 g
Bonsoy: 6.5 g
Soy Life (original): 6.2 g
Sanitarium So Good (regular): 5 g
Australia's Own Organic: 5 g (of organic sugar, of course!)
So Natural (original): 4 g
Soya King: 2.5 g

Eliminating soy milk doesn't mean that milk is completely off the menu for those who are lactose-intolerant, however. Rice milk is a kind of grain milk processed from rice. It is usually made from brown rice and is generally sweet enough without added sugar. The sweetness in most rice milk varieties is generated by an enzymatic process that turns the long chains of glucose molecules (which is what rice largely is) into sugars, especially glucose. Some rice milk varieties may still be sweetened with sugar, so take a close look at the ingredients list to make sure there is none added. The label will say it is about 4 per cent sugar but this is normally just glucose. If sucrose is listed, then the milk contains fructose and you should avoid it. The ingredients list should consist of water, rice, oil and salt (no sugar).

Increasingly, enzyme-treated cow's milk is also becoming available for the lactose-intolerant. Pauls Zymil is an example of one such milk. These milks have been modified by introducing the enzyme for chopping up lactose into the manufacturing process. The lactose comes pre-digested as galactose and glucose (the two sugars which combine to make lactose). This means that lactose-intolerant people need no longer worry about their lack of enzymes; they can once again drink milk with the rest of us.

The only other major category of non-alcoholic drinks you are likely to have in the fridge are sports drinks and their less sporty cousins, 'vitamin waters' and 'energy drinks'. All are sweetened with sugar and must be shown the door. They generally have slightly less sugar than soft drinks, but they still carry a significant sugary punch. There is one important exception, which may become very useful as you try to wean yourself off fructose. Lucozade Original (and *only* the original) is sweetened with pure glucose instead of sugar. If you are of my vintage (over 40), you'll probably remember your mother offering Lucozade when you had a cold (it came in a large orange bottle). It can still be bought in the sports drink section of the local supermarket, but now it comes in smaller (more expensive) bottles. Only the one labelled 'Original' is sweetened with glucose; all the other flavours (and there are many) are sweetened with sugar just like the rest of the drinks you will find on those shelves.

If you are attempting to bring children along on this sugar-free ride with you, it might be worth getting some Lucozade Original; when we took off on this path, we occasionally offered it to our kids and they enjoyed it. It tastes like a not-so-sweet lemonade.

Glucose-sweetened foods and drinks are perfectly acceptable substitutes for the recovering sugarholic. As I've said, sugar is one-half glucose and one-half fructose, but it is only the fructose half that is dangerous to us. Glucose is our fuel source. Our brain cannot run on anything other than pure glucose and every carbohydrate and protein (that is not used to build stuff) is converted to glucose before we use it for energy. We are perfectly adapted to control how much glucose we eat and our appetite control system will accurately monitor every calorie of glucose we ingest. Glucose is the perfect substitute for sugar for the recovering sugarholic. There is, however, a warning about substituting glucose for sugar:

Do not eat foods sweetened with glucose until you have completed withdrawal from sugar.

While you are still eating sugar, your appetite control system is still broken. If significant quantities of fructose are still in your diet, then eating glucose-sweetened foods will make the problem worse, not better. Glucose is metabolised fast and makes its way quickly into the bloodstream. If your apetite control system is broken, any food will cause you to overproduce insulin in a desperate attempt to clear the accumulation of blood sugar. Eating glucose in this state will simply add (extraordinarily efficiently) to the blood sugar load and encourage even more overproduction of insulin. For this reason, you must not substitute glucose until you are certain your appetite control system is operating normally. (You will know when it is – see **Butter and margarine**, pages 114–16.) So, lock up the

Lucozade if you have it. You will be able to drink it when you are through withdrawal, but not before you reach that stage

Powdered drinks

There's one last category of non-alcoholic drinks you need to remove from the pantry – and it is perhaps the most dangerous. Powdered drinks are sold as food for toddlers, 'healthy' afternoon snacks for teenagers and diet drinks for adults. All of them contain significant amounts of fructose and must be thrown out.

Toddler formulas

By toddler formulas, I mean formulas for children older than 12 months. In Australia, formulas for children aged less than 12 months are prohibited by law from containing sucrose (cane sugar). This is not the case in other countries (particularly the US), so pay careful attention to the labels for all formulas if you are reading this anywhere other than Australia or New Zealand.

If you have young children and want to avoid turning them into sugarholics, you need to check the labels on toddler formulas. Until very recently, most manufacturers quite happily filled the formula with cane sugar, in an attempt to convince toddlers to drink what would otherwise be pretty unpalatable stuff. (In some cases, almost half the powder was pure sugar.) There is now a concerted move by manufacturers to replace sugar with glucose in most toddler formulas. As at the date of publication, the only Australian manufacturer still using sugar in toddler formula was Bellamy's in their Organic Toddler Milk. (They use organic sugar, of course, but that doesn't mean it's chemically any different from plain old garden-variety sugar.) That may have changed by the time you are reading this, so check the label. If you see 'organic sugar' (or just 'sugar') on the ingredients list, then out it goes.

Powdered flavouring

No self-respecting four-year-old would drink toddler formula, so the food manufacturers produce 'fun' powdered drinks instead. None of the restraint now being shown in the toddler market is evident in the milk-flavouring market. Powdered milk flavours all contain significant quantities of cane sugar and should all end up in the pile you are taking out to the bin.

Popular Australian toddler formulas
Wyeth has recently removed the sugar (sucrose) from S-26 Gold Toddler and replaced it with lactose. If you have the old formula, toss it; if not, feel free to keep it.
Heinz Nuture Gold Toddler is now sweetened with glucose and lactose, so you can use this.
Nutricia Karicare Gold Plus is now also sweetened with glucose rather than sugar – fine to use.
Nestlé NAN Pro 3 does not contain sugar but its predecessor, Nestlé Neslac Toddler Gold, is almost half sugar, so if you have any old tins in the cupboard, out they go.
Bellamy Organic Toddler contains (organic) cane sugar – out.

Children's milk flavours
Nesquik Strawberry is 98.8% sugar, Banana is 98.2% and Chocolate is 80.7% sugar. Nesquick Plus is 'only' 60% sugar.
Ovaltine is 59% sugar.
Nestlé Milo is 46.4% sugar. The Malt version is slightly better at 45% sugar. And Milo B-Smart is even better with 31.8% sugar.
Note: Most of these concoctions contain lactose as well as sucrose (cane sugar), so the actual amount of sugar in them will be slightly lower than the numbers from the labels. That being said, they are all still very high in sugar.

Adults like powdered drinks, too. Flavoured coffee powders (and syrups) and diet shakes have become very popular in the last few years. Neither of these has a place in a recovering sugarholic's pantry. Coffee flavours like Nestlé's Coffee-Mate range are representative of this type of add-in and are about one-third sugar. Diet shakes are even worse. Most powdered diet shake drinks are sweetened with pure fructose. The recipe varies a little between brands but the typical shake is one-third protein and almost half sugar, with just a smidgeon of fat for taste (in other words, powdered milk plus sugar plus multivitamins). Mixed in accordance with the directions, one meal replacement shake could contain up to 25 g of sugar.

A serving of Coca-Cola the same size as one of these shakes (when mixed) contains about the same amount of sugar. But because Coke uses table sugar (only half fructose) rather than pure fructose, it might find itself in the unusual position of being the healthier alternative. You would need to drink almost twice as much Coke to get the same amount of fructose as is in the average weight-loss shake!

Alcohol

It will sound strange and boring before you give up sugar, but now when I want a drink, I drink water (or sometimes milk). If that doesn't appeal, then I'm not thirsty and don't need a drink. But the same thing does not apply to alcoholic drinks, which we all know we rarely drink because we are thirsty.

The alcohol in wine is created by fermenting the sugars in grape juice (glucose, fructose and sucrose). The alcohol in beer is fermented maltose (maltose is two molecules of glucose joined together). Alcohol (or, more technically, ethanol) is a sugar that has been fermented. A dry wine contains barely any of the original sugar, but a sweet wine such as a botrytis or dessert wine still contains significant amounts of sugar; on average, sweet wines are about 4 per cent fructose.

With one important condition (which I will shortly explain), alcoholic drinks are okay for the recovering sugarholic as long as they don't taste sweet and they are not mixed with other drinks that contain sugar. You can keep the dry wines, beers and spirits, but you need to toss out the dessert wines, ports, sweet sherries, liqueurs and mixers (unless they are diet mixers).

Type of wine	Average sugar content
Average red wine	0.6%
Average white wine	1.0%
Average non-alcoholic wine	1.1%
Dry dessert wine	1.1%
Champagne	1.7%
Sweet dessert wine	7.8%

The important condition is that while alcohol is not part of a sugar addiction, it is of course addictive in its own right. And one of the things that more recent studies (such as the Princeton study mentioned on p. 28) have shown is that lab animals (rats) have a propensity to swap one addiction for another. You will need to guard against the possibility of jumping out of the sugarholic frying pan and into the alcoholic fire. The other important thing to know about alcohol is that it too is metabolised very quickly to fat. Indeed, sugar is almost as efficient at being converted to circulating fat after it is fermented to ethanol as it is before. The chemical pathways are slightly different but the creation of fat is still a direct outcome of alcohol consumption. When you are a sugarholic *and* a drinker, this can result in an acceleration of problems relating to sugar consumption. You will get fatter quicker and you will accelerate towards all of the diseases related to being overweight at a much greater rate. This is because you are layering occasional (fat-creating) alcohol consumption on top of minute-by-minute (fat-creating) fructose consumption.

Some researchers have suggested that fructose is just as dangerous after it has been fermented to ethanol as it is beforehand. They point to similarities in the metabolism of ethanol by the liver and similarities in the outcome of long-term consumption. Alcoholics get cirrhosis of the liver and so do sugarholics. Alcoholics are prone to gout and so are sugarholics. Alcoholics get fat around the stomach and so do sugarholics.

But although these parallels exist, the science suggests that the body actually treats ethanol like any other food rather than in the special way it treats fructose. In fact, a significant number of studies suggest that, in limited quantities, alcohol acts to reduce the effects of fructose. Alcohol consumption has been definitively shown to reduce heart-disease risk factors and help with clearing fats from the arteries. Alcohol stimulates insulin production, just like glucose. This means that our appetite control systems are fully functioning and monitoring the calories from alcohol. There is no fructose-like loophole for alcohol. If you drink, then your body will count the alcohol as food. If your appetite control system is functioning (that is, not stuffed up by fructose) then you will not overeat and the alcohol calories will stop you eating something else. That said, alcohol is addictive and a severe addiction may lead to the consumption of nothing but alcohol. In those sorts of quantities, you will do some of the damage you would otherwise do with fructose.

Once you have eliminated fructose from your diet, the occasional alcoholic drink will not do any significant damage, and some of the research suggests it will actually assist with arterial health.

In this way, alcohol consumption is similar to eating whole fruit: the occasional piece will not do any real damage (in an otherwise fructose-free diet) and it may do some good. If, however, you were to start consuming alcohol at the rate you previously consumed fructose (up to 100 g per day – which equates to approximately 20 standard drinks per day), then you will not have improved your lot at all; you will merely have changed one deadly addiction for another. Even if there are slightly fewer ways to die from alcoholism than obesity, I don't regard this as a step forward. You should aim to have no more than one standard drink (5 g of ethanol) per day once you have gone fructose-free.

Breakfast cereals

Before World War II, breakfast cereals were only eaten by people as a 'digestive aid'. If you were having a little trouble keeping things moving downstairs, then the doctor would suggest you consider cereal for breakfast rather than your usual lambs fry or mutton chops. Needless to say, the breakfast cereal market was not exactly going gangbusters. Competing with a cooked breakfast was always going to be a struggle for cereal makers if the only thing they had going for them was a swift passage.

The war changed many things but perhaps the biggest changes were those associated with the mass entry of women into the work-force. In the extreme circumstances of a world war, traditional gender roles were thrown out and women were encouraged to take over the jobs previously dominated by men. When the men returned from the front, the women often stayed at work. With both adults in the house frequently working at least some of the time, the cooked breakfast quickly became a weekend luxury. You didn't have to hit a manufacturer over the head with a cereal box for them to realise a real market opportunity was developing. The range of cereals quickly blossomed and the ease of preparation became a major theme in breakfast cereal advertising. However, the real leap forward didn't happen until almost the end of the 1940s.

In 1949, a US cereal company (Post) created the first cereal targeted at children. Sugar Crisps were sold as the delicious treat that kids could have for breakfast or straight out of the box for a snack. Sugar was unabashedly the primary ingredient and the sugar arms race began in earnest. Kellogg's jumped on the bandwagon in 1953 with Sugar Smacks (56% sugar). They quickly followed up the success of Sugar Smacks with Apple Jacks (48% sugar) and Froot Loops (42% sugar).

The kids raised on sugar cereals in the fifties became the parents of the seventies. They had been trained to look for cereals that

The 10 lowest-sugar breakfast cereals		
1	**Carman's** Premium Traditional Oats **Freedom Foods** Quick Oats **Coles Smart Buy** Oat Bran, Quick Oats & Rolled Oats	0.0%
2	**Woolworths Select** Rolled Oats	0.6%
3	**Woolworths Home Brand** Semolina	0.7%
4	**Woolworths Select** Quick Cooking Oats **Colest Smart Buy** Wheat Biscuits	0.8%
5	**Nestlé Uncle Tobys** Original Quick Oat Satchets **Lowan** Rice Flakes	0.9%
6	**Nestlé Uncle Tobys** Traditional Oats, Quick Oats, Oat Brits & Vita Brits Weeties **Woolworths Home Brand** Oat Bran	1.0%
7	**Nestlé Uncle Tobys** Vita Brits (Original & Organic)	1.2%
8	**Freedom Foods** Yeast Free Muesli	1.4%
9	**Lowan** Oatbran	1.5%
10	**Sanitarium** Puffed Wheat **Lowan** Quick Oats & Rolled Oats	1.7%

tasted sweet, and the manufacturers of adult cereals were happy to oblige. Almost all cereals now sold in Australia contain significant amounts of sugar. The only cereals that contain even remotely acceptable levels of sugar are variations on (unflavoured) oats and wheat biscuits (provided, of course, you don't add sugar or honey yourself). You'd have to eat eight Weet-bix Kids (number 16 on the lowest-sugar list at 3 per cent sugar) before you even got near one whole teaspoon of sugar. If any of the cereals in the lowest-sugar 10 are in your cupboard now, leave them there. Everything with more than 3 g of sugar per 100 g should be added to the rubbish pile.

The usual suspects fill up the list of cereals with the highest amount of sugar. One small bowl (50 g) of Cocoa Puffs from Coles' or Woolworths' home brands will deliver over five teaspoons of sugar. Not all cereals weigh the same for a given volume (a bowl of corn flakes will be lighter than the same size bowl of muesli). But for most cereals, 50 g is about the amount a child would consume;

The 10 highest-sugar breakfast cereals		
1	Woolworths Home Brand Cocoa Puffs	44.0%
2	Kellogg's Froot Loops	41.7%
3	Kellogg's Frosties	41.3%
4	Coles Cocoa Puffs	39.5%
5	Kellogg's Coco Pops	36.7%
6	Nestlé Uncle Tobys Oats Temptations Sultanas, Apple & Honey	34.0%
7	Kellogg's Nutrigrain and Coco Pops Chex	32.0%
8	Nestlé Nesquick Kellogg's Crunchy Nut Corn Flakes	31.7%
9	Kellogg's Crunchy Nut Corn Flakes Nutty	31.3%
10	Kellogg's Just Right Original	31.1%

for an adult's portion, doubling the amount of sugar will give you a good idea of what you're consuming.

People who believe the health-food marketing messages of the cereal makers might be a bit surprised by some of the entries in the highest-sugar list. If you see honey or sultanas in the name of a cereal, it's usually a good idea to check the sugar content carefully. Don't be fooled by the branding of new ranges of flavoured oat cereals, either. Unlike their unflavoured cousins, they are usually extremely high in sugar. One (adult-sized) 100 g serve of Uncle Tobys Oat Temptations (Sultanas, Apple & Honey flavour) will parachute eight teaspoons (34 g) of sugar into your diet. A complete listing of all cereals is available from www.HowMuchSugar.com.

Muesli and snack bars

You are about to significantly reduce your children's lunchbox options. Almost all muesli and snack bars contain extraordinarily high amounts of sugar. However, not all bars are created equal. Some are 30 g and some are 70 g and there are lots in between. To make sure we're comparing apples with apples, I've expressed the sugar content as a percentage, but I've also added some columns that show you how much sugar you will get in the whole bar.

Although these (see page 74) are the lowest-sugar bars available, I wouldn't be feeding any of these to my kids (or me), with the possible exception of the Go Natural nut bars and the two Carman's bars. The Go Natural and Carman's bars are low in sugar (but could be better) and are not artificially sweetened. While I don't consider artificial sweeteners to be worse than fructose for short-term getting-unaddicted-to-sugar use, I wouldn't recommend them for long-term consumption and certainly wouldn't want to start my kids on a lifetime habit.

The highest-sugar muesli and snack bars listed opposite should be classified as confectionery, but unfortunately they are all too often marketed as healthy alternatives, particularly for children. Just for fun, I've included something that is marketed as confectionery (the Mars Bar), to show where it would sit in the list. It also illustrates how the serving size can significantly alter the perceived amount of sugar. Children are unlikely to stop at one 'fun size' Mars Bar and are equally likely to stop at one tube of a Fruit Fix pack (the recommended serving size). Nevertheless, on a straight comparison of teaspoons of sugar per serve, the Mars Bar comes out as one of the best in this list (at 'only' 2.5 teaspoons of sugar per bar).

	Bar	% sugar	Bar size (g)	Sugar in bar (tsp)
	The 10 lowest-sugar muesli and snack bars			
1	**Atkins** Advantage range	0.0–5.0*	60	0.00
2	**Go Natural** Nut Clusters range	3.7–4.0	30	0.25
3	**Carman's** Original Fruit-free	7.1	45	0.75
4	**Carman's** Apricot & Almond	8.2	45	1.00
5	**Slim Secrets** range	8.5–11.0#^	40	1.00
6	**Be Natural** Honey Nut Trail Bar	13.1	32	1.00
7	**100 Healthy Calories** Super Berry Breakfast Bar	13.4	35	1.25
8	**Weight Watchers** Ginger Kiss Muffin Bar	14.0^	35	1.25
9	**A.O.** Mixed Nut Bar	14.3	35	1.25
10	**Be Natural** Sunflower & Pepita Nut Bar	14.5	60	2.00

* Sweetened with sucralose (short-term use probably not damaging – see chapter 4)
# Sweetened with maltitol (as bad as sugar – see chapter 4)
^ Sweetened with polydextrose (as bad as sugar – see chapter 4)

	Bar	% sugar	Bar size (g)	Sugar in bar (tsp)
	The 10 highest-sugar muesli and snack bars			
1	**Uncle Tobys** Fruit Fix Range	71.6–73.9	21.6	4.00
2	**Mars** Fun Size	58.5	18	2.50
3	**Sun** Apricot Bar	57.2	50	7.00
4	**Go Natural** All Fruit range	55.1–56.2	35	4.50
5	**Go Natural** Popcorn & Fruit Bar range	51.4–53.8	35	4.50·
6	**Go Natural** Sesame Crisp	45.0	40	4.50
7	**Be Natural** Fruit & Nut Bar (yoghurt-coated)	44.6	50	5.25
8	**Orgran** Fruit Filled Blueberry Bar	43.0	50	5.25
9	**Sun** Cashew Nut & Honey Bar	42.9	35	3.50
10	**Tasti** Snak Log – Carob, Fruit & Nut	42.5	40	4.00
11	**Coles Smart Buy** Choc Chip Chewy Muesli Bar	41.2	25	2.50

Condiments

I'd be very surprised if a single condiment in your cupboard had less than 15 per cent sugar, and I'd wager most are way over 20 per cent. Commercial sauces (barbecue and tomato) can all go in the bin. And mayo can follow, unless it is whole-egg full-fat. You can keep the soy sauce and the taco sauce but the rest is pure trouble. Take a look at chapter 3 for a detailed guide to some of the alternatives to the commercial products you are tossing in the bin.

Yoghurt

If you have yoghurt in your fridge, it is very likely to be high in sugar. This is a trap for new players. For the longest time, I purchased yoghurt on the understanding that when they say 'No added sugar' on the label, it means no added sugar. I eventually discovered that this is not exactly true. I was buying the Jalna range of fruit yoghurts because they were emblazoned with that phrase. When the slogan suddenly changed to 'No added cane sugar', the red lights started flashing. Peering closely at the ingredients list, I found that there was indeed no cane sugar, but I noticed that 'fruit juice extract' was pretty high on the list. Fruit juice extract or concentrate is just another phrase which can be translated as 'sugar'. Sugar molecules are no less dangerous because they were once part of a piece of fruit than they are having once been part of sugar cane. When I looked at an old yoghurt container, with the original 'No added sugar' terminology, I discovered, to my despair, that all the ingredients were exactly the same. The only change was the (probably legally inspired) insertion of the word 'cane' into the proud boast on the front of the label. I was aghast. I had been feeding my kids this stuff believing it to be sugar-free and it was nothing of the sort. No wonder they gobbled it up like it was ice-cream.

In its natural state, yoghurt is extremely tart. If what you have in the fridge is anything other than sour-tasting, then it has been sweetened with something – either sugar, pure fructose (often described as 'concentrated fruit juice' on the label) or an artificial sweetener. Like milk, yoghurt contains lactose, so you need to adjust the sugar figure on the label to work out how much fructose you're getting. In the tables opposite, I have assumed that lactose accounts for 4.7 g per 100 g of the sugars listed on the label. Besides lactose, most of the sugar in yoghurt is added fructose or sugars associated with the fruit flavourings. If the sweetener being used is 'concentrated fruit juice', it is pure fructose, so, you can safely double the estimated number of teaspoons. Treat the tables as the minimum amount of sugar you will get in the product. The percentages have been calculated by using the 'sugars' amount on the label and subtracting 4.7 g per 100 g for lactose. (i.e. When I say that Jalna Biodynamic Fat Free has no sugar, I mean that it's label says it has 4.7 per cent sugar. But since that is exactly the amount of lactose that unsweetened yoghurt contains, I've listed

The 10 lowest-sugar yoghurts		
1	Jalna Biodynamic Fat Free	0.0%
2	Nestlé Diet Range	0.1–0.9%*^
3	Yoplait formé Range	0.4–1.1%*^
4	Jalna Genuine Leben European Style	0.5%
5	Pauls Ideal Natural	0.6%
6	Jalna Fat Free Natural	0.8%
7	Jalna Whole Milk Natural	0.9%
8	Dairy Farmers European Style	1.1%
9	Jalna Biodynamic Whole Milk	1.3%
10	Dairy Farmers Traditional	1.6%

Sweetened with acesulphame potassium* and aspartame^ (see Figure 4.1, page 170)

The 10 highest-sugar yoghurts		
1	Ski Double-Up Range	17.6–13.3%
2	Nestlé All Natural Muesli Cup Range	15.0–12.3%
3	Ski D'Lite Honey Buzz	13.8%
4	Vaalia Low Fat Lemon Crème	13.4%
5	Vaalia Vanilla on Lemon Crème	12.8%
6	Yoplait Go-Gurt Range	12.8–12.2%
7	Yoplait Smackers Range	12.6–12.0%
8	Nestlé Real Fruit Range	12.4–11.2%
9	Yoplait Lite French Cheesecake	12.4%
10	Pauls Lite Vanilla	12.1%

it as 0 per cent because it has no sugars that concern recovering sugarholics.)

Besides the diet yoghurts, none of the 10 lowest-sugar varieties will taste sweet and all of them are perfectly acceptable to recovering sugarholics. Eating sour yoghurt is not my idea of fun, but it does form a great base for salad dressing.

If you have any of the yoghurts in the highest-sugar table in your fridge, do not detain them on their way to the bin.

Yoghurt is quite heavy, so while 12 per cent sugar doesn't look that bad, remember that a small tub is around 200 g. That means that a small tub of Pauls Lite Vanilla yoghurt will deliver 24.2 g of sugar. Or, put another way, you'll be consuming just under six teaspoons of sugar in your small tub of yoghurt. If you're eating the highest-sugar variation of the Ski Double-Up range, you'll be gobbling up over eight teaspoons of sugar in that tiny tub. Would you like some yoghurt with your sugar?

Ice-cream

You won't be surprised to find that you've got to clean out all your ice-creams. Even a small bowl (200 g) of the lowest-sugar ice-cream delivers two teaspoons of sugar as well as several artificial sweeteners. And that's not even taking account of the fact that one of the sweeteners (sorbitol) is essentially metabolised as fructose anyway (see chapter 4). You'll be pleased to discover that I do provide a great recipe for sugar-free ice-cream in chapter 5. (Ice-cream made from glucose is almost identical to ice-cream made from sugar. Unfortunately, however, you have to make it yourself; no manufacturer yet makes ice-cream this way.) The percentages used in the tables opposite have been calculated by using the 'sugars' amount on the label and subtracting 4.7 g for lactose in the appropriate products.

One rounded scoop of ice-cream from a standard ice-cream

	The 10 lowest-sugar ice-creams	
1	Nestlé Peters No Sugar Added	4.0%*
2	Gelati Italia Yolati Range (Mango, Raspberry or Baci)	6.6–7.0%
3	Norgen Vaaz Vanilla Supreme	10.8%
4	Connoisseur Maple Pecan Pie	11.9%
5	Bulla Chocolate Lights	12.0%
6	Streets Thickshake Paddle Pop	12.3%
7	Streets Golden Gaytime Bulla Lights (English Toffee or Mango)	12.4%
8	Bulla 98% Fat Free Vanilla	12.5%
9	Coles You'll Love Coles Reduced Fat Vanilla	12.6%
10	Norgen Vaaz Strawberry Summer and Vanilla Choc Fudge Bulla Strawberry Milky Pops	12.7%

*The Peters 'no sugar added' ice-cream is sweetened with sorbitol and polydextrose. In my opinion this rules it out of contention as the number one ice-cream product because of the way these two artificial sweeteners are digested (see chapter 4 for more detail on why). It gets the number one spot on a technicality.

	The 10 highest-sugar ice-creams	
1	Streets Blue Ribbon Parlour Style Choc Chip Swirl	48.6%
2	Streets Blue Ribbon Parlour Style (Caramel Fudge Twist, Minty Choc Flake or Strawberries and Cream)	46.4%
3	Sara Lee Honeycomb & Butterscotch	43.2%
4	Streets Blue Ribbon Parlour Style Cookies and Cream	42.0%
5	Cadbury Raspberry Triple Decker	41.2%
6	Sara Lee Rocky Road Overload	39.5%
7	Sara Lee Absolutely Raspberry	34.7%
8	Nestlé Peters Smarties Cone	34.0%
9	Sara Lee French Vanilla	32.6%
10	Connoisseur Mint Seduction	32.0%

scooper is 100 g. Since most people would be eating at least two scoops of ice-cream (unless we're paying a fortune for 'gourmet' cuisine), you can double the percentages in these tables to get a feel for how much sugar you'd be eating. For example, two scoops of the Gelati Italia range will give you about 14 g of (non-lactose) sugar. That's around 3 teaspoons – and it's one of the lowest-sugar products!

None of this really matters when you can't eat any ice-creams bought in a shop. But I've listed the 10 lowest-sugar and highest-sugar varieties on page 79, for your interest. One 200 g serve (two scoops) of Streets Blue Ribbon will give you a huge 23 teaspoons of sugar.

Step 4 – Withdrawal

Walt Disney once said, 'The way to get started is to quit talking and begin doing.' And that is the point at which we have arrived on our mission to break your sugar addiction.

There's nothing fun about the withdrawal period, but it does end. And once it does, you'll be completely free from the desire to eat sugar ever again. A plate of bikkies will hold all the attraction of a plate of raw broccoli. This is because addiction works by developing a reward-and-punishment system. As soon as you stop taking the addictive substance, its euphoric effect begins to decline, creating a mild depression in the process. It feels like an emptiness, or even a boredom. It doesn't hurt but as it accumulates, it makes you crave the hit that you know will relieve it. Eating sugar in moderation for the rest of your life is the worst of all worlds. You're not eating enough to truly relieve the craving (and so no reward for you), but you are eating enough to maintain the dopamine response that keeps the addiction circuit alive in your brain. They don't get heroin addicts off the 'gear' by hooking them on a smaller dose of heroin, and you won't get unaddicted to sugar by eating a smaller dose forever, either. I'm horrified by pharmaceutical companies that have convinced smokers to become addicted to lifelong supplies of their nicotine patches rather than lifelong supplies of cigarettes. Surely the aim should be to help them break their nicotine addiction. This is not to say that you necessarily must go 'cold turkey' (as I did) in order to become unaddicted. A sudden stop works well for some people but others find it easier to ratchet down their consumption until they are no longer addicted. I go into this in more detail a little later on (see page 87).

The way to become unaddicted to sugar is to start *today*. You can't drift into stopping an addiction. Because your lust for sugar is a chemical addiction, there will be a chemical withdrawal. And that is not going to be pleasant. You have been addicted to fructose since before you could talk, so getting unaddicted will take a modicum of effort and a couple of bright-line rules. What it will not take is willpower.

If you are going cold turkey, I suggest having a last supper of your favourite sugary treat. Get that Mars Bar or that can of Coke. Sit down and consciously enjoy the very last time in your life that you will eat (or drink) sugar. Really enjoy it, right down to the last morsel. Enjoy the pleasure of a full-blown addiction response as the dopamine and the endorphins course through your brain. Now stop. You will henceforth not touch a food containing sugar. This will not be fun, at first. But starting is half the battle. Hold the line. There is no moderation. You have stopped poisoning yourself. If you can just get past the next few weeks of danger, you will enjoy the health sugar has sucked from your life to date.

Then, all of a sudden, your desire for sugar will vanish. I know it sounds strange, but it just plain goes. Bang! And you will never want the stuff again. It's hard to make it sound believable until you have experienced it for yourself (you have, after all, spent your life addicted to this substance and known no other reality), but it really does happen.

What will withdrawal be like?

Withdrawal is different for everybody. It lasts different amounts of time and it feels different. Almost every person I have spoken to since the release of *Sweet Poison* has a different withdrawal story. Some people say they didn't really notice it. Perhaps they felt unwell for a day or two but that quickly passed and then they didn't like sugar any more. But these people are very much the exception. We all have different levels of susceptibility to addiction. Some people can indeed have just one cigarette or the occasional puff. The same goes for sugar. Some people (and I am not one of them) can happily indulge in the occasional sugar hit and suffer no addiction. From what I can gather, my experience is more typical. Most of us are genuinely addicted. When we stop taking the addictive substance, we go through withdrawal and if we ever expose ourselves to it again (in quantity) we become addicted again. If you are a person who can take or leave sugar, then congratulations, you've got it easy. All you need to do is make sure you don't eat too much of it. Just because you're not addicted doesn't mean that sugar is not doing damage; it just means you can push down your intake much more easily than the rest of us.

For everyone else, here's what to expect during withdrawal. In the first few days I was continuously hungry, no matter what I ate (as long as it didn't contain sugar). I could not walk past the jar of nuts I'd placed in the kitchen without having a handful. I could not say no to food. I wanted it all the time. I let myself go with the flow; I made sure I didn't eat sugar, but I sure ate a lot of everything else. I now know that what I was experiencing was that kind of mild dissatisfied feeling that isn't true hunger at all. Rather, it was what I had come to know as 'hunger' after so many years addicted to sugar. Sugarholics rarely feel true gut-grinding hunger and they rarely feel genuinely full. Their appetite control is stuck at half-on (or half-off) and they are always sort of up for a meal, especially if sugar is involved. After withdrawal, I came to know what hunger really feels like, and what I was feeling at the start of withdrawal was more of a nagging desire for (preferably sweet) food. If I ate food, it didn't help at all. No sooner was the last mouthful sliding down my throat than I was 'on the tooth' again, thinking about my next meal. It wasn't painful, just mildly unpleasant. This is the mechanism of addiction that drives you to seek out the addictive substance. I largely resisted but, on one occasion, in a social situation, I vividly remember succumbing.

I was out at one of those formal dinners where the waiters come around and serve alternating meals. (One of those where you inevitably end up with dinner envy, wishing you'd got the steak instead of the unidentifiable battered mound piled decoratively on your plate.) Dessert time arrived. In a restaurant situation, I would simply not order dessert, thereby avoiding any potential sugar temptation during withdrawal. But here, the dessert (a scrumptious dark-chocolate layer cake) was placed in front of me while I was looking the other way (truly!). There I was staring it down as all the other guests started eating and told me how tasty it was. What can it hurt?, I thought to myself, and tucked in. It was tasty. It was *very* tasty. I didn't stop at just one mouthful, either. I was practically licking the plate. That vague, gnawing hunger-like feeling disappeared for the first time in days and I felt great. I kept feeling great until the next morning, when the hunger-like feeling came back, a headache developed and I really, really wanted something sweet for breakfast.

Luckily, by this time I had recognised my addiction for what it was and was determined not to let it get the better of me. I stayed off the sugar from that point forward and eventually came out the other side. The sugar did indeed cure my withdrawal symptoms temporarily but I suspect that having the hit wheeled me back to square one.

Opioid withdrawal symptoms

The little research there is on sugar addiction points to it affecting the brain in the same manner as the opioid class of drugs. This includes drugs such as opium, morphine, codeine, methadone and endorphins (generated when we exercise). Opioid addiction is quite different from alcohol dependence, which relies on a different physical mechanism.

The research on opioid withdrawal syndrome suggests you can expect to experience some or all of the following symptoms when withdrawing from an addiction to an opioid:

1. Yawning
2. Sweating
3. Streaming eyes and runny nose
4. Dilated pupils
5. Anxiety
6. Restlessness
7. Insomnia
8. Chills
9. Tachycardia (accelerated heartbeat)
10. Hypertension
11. Nausea or vomiting
12. Crampy abdominal pains and possibly diarrhoea
13. Muscle aches and pains

Unlike withdrawal from alcohol, opioid withdrawal is not life-threatening and you may not experience all of these symptoms. It is not painful to withdraw from sugar. For me, the main symptom was a gnawing craving, with occasional (and largely mild) bouts of other symptoms (like headache).

The other charming symptom of this part of the withdrawal was that I seemed to have a perpetual (but not severe) headache. That ugly, headachey, hungry part of the withdrawal lasted another three days – and I had been three days in when I ate the chocolate cake. I believe that had I not had the cake, that part would have passed more quickly. By taking the sugar, I reinforced the feedback loop that was keeping the reward circuits in my brain under the control of fructose (or, probably more accurately, cortisol generated by fructose).

All through this part of the withdrawal (approximately the first week), I felt under the weather, and if many others had not reported similar experiences, I might have attributed them to a mild head cold. While I don't recall this, those who were around me assure me that definite mood swings were involved, and maybe even a bit of crankiness. (Who could blame me? I was hungry and had a head-ache.) Fortunately for me (and them), this phase didn't last long. Two or three days after the chocolate cake incident, it shifted to a complete lack of hunger. And I mean complete! Even at the times I would normally have been hungry (or at least habitually eating), there was nothing.

I still, however, had a very strong desire for sugar and would catch myself seeking it out. The habits I had spent so many years developing around sugar consumption were not helping, either. This is where you will be very glad of the avoidance strategies you developed at **Step 2**. Avoid the situations in which you habitu-ally consumed sugar and you will be a long way towards defeating the addiction. This will not stop you wanting a sweet taste in your mouth, but it will stop you walking into situations without a strat-egy (like I did with the chocolate cake).

What withdrawal was like (from the Sweet Poison Forum) . . .

Well, after my initial excitement, I must say I am struggling a bit. Now on about day 17. The first week I felt terrible with headaches but excited because I could feel the weight loss happening. The second week it was still that way, but less aches and pains. Now, for the last five days, I have had headaches again – and I feel a bit down.

And later . . .

I lost two kilos in two weeks and then for a month – nothing. I only had about six kilos to lose and I felt [further] weight loss would be insignificant.

I can't tell you the number of occasions I have said no to sugar. This week we were working on a show featuring honey and choco-late and all sorts of sweet stuff – the food provided as snacks was all sugar, bar one savoury option. I did feel a bit hard done by as I kept having to excuse myself from eating any of it.

I was rewarded with another kilo lost! It's strange how you don't lose anything for a month and then, one day, off it goes. I feel that is a great signal of encouragement and worth the wait.

And quite some time later . . .

Hi all! Thought I'd let you know my progress; it's been a while. Have lost four kilos now, after five months, but then didn't have so much to lose. The thing that surprises me most is how 'compact' I am – not sure how else to put it! I feel not only slimmer but firmer. My daughter said perhaps when you cut out sugar you reduce bloating, which would make you feel firmer.

Anyway, just spent a month away and was confronted every day with lovely homemade cakes and sweets etc. I did not touch one! Everyone asked me my secret and I talked about *Sweet*

Poison, but they seemed more interested in the shakes or whatever to lose kilos FAST, while they all devoured the sweets in front of them.

The best part of all is I did not feel at all like I was missing out. There were no cravings – and even better still is that I believe I have conquered the eating-as-a-habit regime. That's what is really making the difference – the desire for sweet made me constantly nibble and now I have gotten used to not putting things in my mouth. Some days I can't believe how little I have eaten without even trying. This is a lifestyle that, once developed, is very easy to maintain.

Vicki J

Going cold turkey

In *Sweet Poison*, I tell of the 'cold turkey' approach I took to sugar. At the time, I wrote that I was basing the success of this approach on a case study of one: me. Now, thousands of people have broken the sugar habit and hundreds have written to tell me of their experiences, and what they say has only strengthened my philosophy. Every person that has told me of going cold turkey has ultimately managed to kick the habit.

To go cold turkey, you will probably need to use substitutes. A major component of my avoidance strategy involved, wherever possible, substituting an artificial sweetener for the sugar I was used to having. In my case, that required a fridge full of Pepsi Max. Whenever I felt the need for sugar, I'd hit the fridge. I switched to Pepsi Max because it was the one cola that tasted (to me) the most like it was sweetened with sugar. I didn't make this decision based on science; at that stage, I hadn't been able to find any evidence that proved conclusively that sugar was addictive. (This was well before the release of the recent studies on the addictive qualities of sugar.) And I certainly didn't know that aspartame (the sweetener used in Pepsi Max) was any less addictive than sugar. I just knew that I had to stop drinking sugar, but that I couldn't get out of the habit of wanting a sweet drink.

I found that swigging Pepsi Max was only partially satisfying. I was in the habit of having a sweet drink whenever I spotted a vending machine or when relaxing on a hot day and, while I was in the depths of sugar withdrawal (headaches, hunger and cravings), the Pepsi did nothing for how under-the-weather I was feeling, but at least it allowed me to continue this habit without consuming fructose.

My Pepsi Max habit lasted about two weeks. I can remember the day I decided it was no longer necessary. I was at the supermarket, about to load another carton of Pepsi Max (on special, no less) into the trolley, when a shocking thought occurred to me: I didn't really like the taste. In the past, I had always preferred full-sugar to the artificial stuff, but artificial had been an acceptable alternative on short notice. Now that I had been drinking it non-stop for two weeks, I realised that I really didn't like the taste. Sure, it was cold and bubbly – and sweet, in a metallic kind of way. But it wasn't doing anything for me. In fact, cold sparkling mineral water sounded more appealing.

Never before in my life had I felt that water would be more appealing than any other beverage. It was quite a shock. Smoking addicts often describe the moment they realised they were no longer addicted as a revelation. And I think that moment in the supermarket, when I placed the carton back on the shelf and reached for the mineral water, was just such a revelation. I actually didn't want sugar!

Since the publication of *Sweet Poison*, hundreds of people have written to me and described a very similar moment of revelation. It might take three weeks or it might take three months, but after a period of consciously keeping yourself away from sugar, you'll suddenly feel no attraction to it at all. You'll be able to stand safely in front of a plate of chocolates and not feel the slightest temptation to have one. There is a note of warning, however. A few people have also written and expressed frustration that, having gone through withdrawal, they have had some sugar only to find themselves well and truly back on the wagon, lusting after it at every turn. They have resigned themselves to another withdrawal period and eventually got through it, but it's not an experience they would recommend to others.

Rule 3: Once a sugarholic, always a sugarholic; you can't afford to have even a little.

Once you are sugar-free, you really can eat anything you like as long as it doesn't contain sugar. Your body will moderate your consumption and keep you on the straight and narrow. Chapter 5 provides recipes for sugar-free treats. However, be aware that you should not use these recipes while you are still consuming fructose (see page 193). They substitute glucose (dextrose) for sugar (glucose + fructose). Glucose is quickly metabolised and raises blood sugar levels fast. The jump in blood sugar will cause a spike in insulin production. If your arteries are full of fat, insulin levels will stay high for a long period as your body attempts to reduce the blood sugar. Unfortunately, the high blood fats will continue to impair your ability to bring blood sugar under control.

Men are from Mars

In *Sweet Poison*, I mentioned research indicating that men and post-menopausal women are the most affected by fructose. I theorised that perhaps what was protecting pre-menopausal women was oestrogen. I based that thinking on a line of research that started with a 1966 study by Dr MacDonald from the Guy's Hospital Medical School in London. Dr MacDonald fed a mixed group of pre- and post-menopausal women and some men solutions that were either glucose- or fructose-loaded. He noticed that the men and post-menopausal women on the fructose diet had increased fatty acids in their blood. This confirmed what rat studies had shown at around the same time: that pre-menopausal women (and rats) were in some way immune to the most dangerous effects of fructose.

A very recent study by the Lausanne University School of Biology and Medicine in Switzerland confirms Dr MacDonald's work but gives even more detailed findings. Not only are circulating fatty acids lower in pre-menopausal women, but these women do not develop insulin-resistance – unlike their male counterparts. The researchers called for more research, given this was a very small and short study. But, interestingly, they speculated that the difference might be that pre-menopausal women appear to be extremely efficient at converting the fatty acids created by fructose into leg (or, more accurately, bottom) fat. This rapid creation of leg fat seems to provide protection against the more dangerous aspects of fructose consumption (insulin-resistance and central adiposity or, as we know it, tummy fat). Something about menopause (and I speculate that it's the sudden decrease in oestrogen) causes women's bodies to start acting like men's when it comes to fructose: they stop storing leg fat, start storing tummy fat and start developing insulin-resistance and blocked arteries. Interestingly, studies of male to female transsexuals reveal exactly the opposite: as soon as the oestrogen hormone therapy starts, fat migrates away from the trunk towards the hips and buttocks. A fat bottom may not be the most desirable thing in the fashion world, but as far as nasty little diseases go, it's much better that the fructose makes its way there than staying in the arteries or accumulating around the waist.

PMT and menopause

I have found with my patients that some, including myself, had PMT symptoms pretty much vanish once fructose was removed from their diet.

Lani (naturopath)

I have been on a very low-fructose intake for six months and have not had a hot flush for at least three of those months. This is somewhat of a miracle for me, after three years of intermittent hot flushes – from one a day sometimes to four an hour other times. This is the first time I have gone months with not a flicker of a flush. Whether it remains that way is to be seen; however, I have never had such a long stint without them.

Vicki J

Sugar and hormones

There appears to be a lot of anecdotal evidence to suggest that it's better for women not to consume sugar during menopause. Various web sites suggest that keeping sugar intake low will reduce the impact of hot flushes and other symptoms. So far, I haven't been able to pin down any reputable scientific source for this thinking. Strangely, male researchers seem disinclined to look too hard at associations between menopause and fructose. But this latest research (pages 89–90) does suggest there is some kind of link between fructose metabolism and pre-menopausal hormones.

Another difficulty that many women face is polycystic ovary syndrome (PCOS). Sometimes referred to as 'hyperandrogen anovulation syndrome' or 'Stein Leventhal Syndrome', it is a hormonal disorder that was first described by doctors in the 1930s. Not much is known about PCOS other than that it appears to be related to insulin-resistance (80 per cent of sufferers are insulin-resistant) and oestrogen production. The syndrome is nevertheless very real – it affects around one in 10 Australian women of childbearing age – and can have a dramatic impact on a young woman's ability to fall pregnant. PCOS appears to push woman to a more male-like hormone orientation. Sufferers develop facial hair and typically gain weight around the abdomen rather than the hips and buttocks. Having PCOS is also a strong risk factor (along with being over-weight and having high blood pressure) for gestational diabetes, should the sufferer manage to fall pregnant.

Gestational diabetes is not a good thing for a growing baby. Just like any other diabetes, it means that the pancreas is unable to pro-duce enough insulin to clear the blood of food. When the mother's pancreas can't keep up, the baby's pancreas becomes a reserve insulin generator. This brand-spanking new pancreas can pump out insulin till the cows come home. All the extra insulin works to convert the mother's excess food to body fat (on the baby), which is why babies of diabetic mums tend to be a lot bigger than average. The downside is that the baby is born with a lot of extra miles already on its pancreas, which ultimately makes it more susceptible to diabetes itself.

The science on PCOS and gestational diabetes is very thin on the ground. These are areas where what we know is significantly outweighed by what we don't. But I can't help drawing some con-nections. We know that the relationship between oestrogen and male hormones (like testosterone) in a woman's body is a very finely balanced array of interactions. We also know that the presence of oestrogen (or the absence of testosterone) is likely to be significantly implicated in the damage done by fructose. Women of childbearing age (post-puberty and pre-menopause) appear to be almost immune to many of the more damaging aspects of eating fructose (except for the looking-bad-in-togs bit). The last thing we know is that women who eat fructose (and become insulin-resistant as a result) are prone to other hormone disorders like PCOS. We don't know how (or even if) fructose metabolism has anything to do with oestrogen and androgen regulation, but from where I'm standing, I'd say it's a good bet. Hormones like these interact in ways we are only just beginning to understand. Introducing something to the diet (in the quantities that we have) that probably interferes significantly with these interactions looks, to me, like a disaster waiting to happen. Since childbirth is a reasonably important part of many women's lives, I propose that cutting out sugar is a worthwhile risk-avoidance strategy for those who are pregnant or those who would like to be.

Things a prospective mum should know:

1. Fructose is likely to be implicated in PCOS, which means it may affect your ability to fall pregnant.
2. Fructose is likely to be implicated in gestational diabetes, which means it may affect your ability to have a healthy pregnancy and a healthy baby.
3. Fructose definitely affects copper metabolism, which can affect collagen and elastin cross-linking in your baby's growing muscles and organs. (This can result in skeletal and joint abnormalities, and vascular lesions that can lead to aneurisms and ruptures.)
4. Fructose definitely affects iodine metabolism, which affects your baby's IQ (and not in a good way).

Is slow withdrawal an option?

Another finding for which I have no scientific evidence is that women find fructose withdrawal significantly more difficult than men. Men seem to be able to go cold turkey and, after a rough week or two, be through withdrawal. Some women report the same experience, but they appear to be in the minority. Many women struggle with sugar cravings for months before they are free of the withdrawal period. And they report that the cravings significantly intensify during menstruation, making it doubly hard to stick to their no-sugar regime. Women also report that withdrawal seems to last longer and be more difficult than what I describe in *Sweet Poison*, and what men in their lives report. They do eventually get to the point of revelation, where sugar has absolutely no attraction, but some report it has taken them up to three months to reach that point. Other women say that they have found it easier to reduce their sugar intake slowly rather than stopping suddenly; in this way, they gradually reduce their desire for it. If you can do that and manage to continuously reduce your intake, then by all means do it. (I couldn't. I had to stop cold, which is why I've included **Rule 3**.) Taking all of this together, it looks like slowly reducing sugar intake may result in a much longer withdrawal period than simply stopping. But if you can't go cold turkey, then gradual reduction will work just as well.

My fructose-reduction program is working well. Feel good, weight falling (8 kg so far), not hard at all. All good.

A few of the guys in the office have been giving it a go (including one very cynical guy who has tried everything under the sun) with the same results. Strangely, I have found women more resistant to the concept than guys. Possibly, women have a greater sweet tooth than men and they find giving up sweetness a step too far.

A couple say, 'Isn't fructose fruit sugar? How can that be bad?' I recently tried a new approach when talking to women about the issue. I simply say that I am 'fructose-intolerant'. As 'lactose-intolerance' is seen as legit by most women, they seem to find the idea of fructose-intolerance more acceptable. But they say they have never heard of that and ask what it is.

I then explain that I can only eat fructose in whole fruit, other-wise I suffer from the following: fatigue, bloating, poor sleep, weight gain, high blood pressure, excessive appetite . . . (i.e. the familiar list of fructose-related maladies). That seems to get through, and you can see the light go on: 'My, that sounds like what I've got!'

Whatever works, I guess.

Paul

I can't find anything in the research to indicate why women tend to find it easier to have a slow withdrawal and men find it eas-ier to stop cold, but the stories I hear are very consistent with this. It may be related to the effects of oestrogen, particularly given the observation that sugar cravings are much worse during menstrua-tion. Or it just might be coincidence. But whatever works best for you is the way to go during withdrawal. I couldn't manage a gradual withdrawal because the temptation would have been too great. But I'm a jump-straight-into-the-cold-pool kind of guy, while my wife, Lizzie, is a slowly-immerse-yourself kind of woman. I think her method is mad and I'm sure she feels the same about mine, but the point is that we both end up in the pool.

Slow-withdrawal caution

The only caution if you are doing the slow withdrawal is: Don't kid yourself. Make sure you are actually reducing your sugar intake con-sistently. Don't have 'just one more for the road', or you'll find that, little by little, your sugar intake will creep back up. The best way to make sure you're reducing is to keep a sugar diary. Note where and how much you consume sugar before you start and set yourself a weekly target of eliminating a few of those sugar sources or amounts.

For example, if you are in the habit of having four cups of tea a day with two teaspoons of sugar in each, cut back to two cups a day in the first week and then cut back first one and then the second teaspoon of sugar over the following weeks. Before you know it, you'll be drinking tea without sugar and you won't even miss it. Or, if you enjoy a cereal like Sultana Bran for breakfast, try buying plain bran and adding a few sultanas. Slowly, over time, reduce the sultana content, until you are adding none. Then buy a lower sugar bran. Once again, you will have slipped into sugar-free breakfast without the sudden withdrawal.

Step 5 – Re-stocking

Once you start withdrawal, you'll need to re-stock your now-bare larder. This step guides you through the sugar-laden minefield that is the modern supermarket.

If you are like most Australians, **Step 3** will have left you with almost nothing in the cupboard, fridge or freezer. You're probably looking at the empty shelves and thinking, 'Brilliant! Gillespie's invented the no-food diet – no wonder he lost weight.' But don't worry, there is a surprisingly large array of very nice food available without any sugar or with very low sugar content. Even within the categories I have told you to purge, there are brands that are very low in sugar; the trick is to choose wisely.

The Fat Theory

Before we go any further, I'd like to bring up the awkward issue of fat. No, not yours and mine, but fat in the food supply. In *Sweet Poison*, I outlined how the theory of 'fat makes you fat' came to be the mantra of nutritionists. The Fat Theory grew from an interesting (but false) deduction from an equally interesting observation. Dr Ancel Keys (the father of the US Army's 'K-rations', used by soldiers in combat) studied the eating habits of 22 countries in the decade after World War II. Heart disease was reaching epidemic proportions in the United States at the time, with almost two out of every three deaths directly attributable to heart failure.

Dr Keys was trying to determine whether there was anything about the US diet that might give a clue as to why heart disease was accelerating out of control. For reasons he never really explained, Dr Keys focused on seven countries. For each country, he plotted the amount of fat in the population's diet against the incidence of death from heart disease. The seven countries he chose fitted very neatly on a line of correlation that Dr Keys said indicated that the more fat in a population's diet, the higher the rate of heart disease. Japan, with a very low-fat diet, had a very low rate of heart disease. The US, with a very high-fat diet, had a very high rate of heart disease. The evidence was accepted hook, line and sinker by the nutritionists and the governments for which they worked. It is, after all, highly intuitive that eating fat would fill your arteries with fat, and it wasn't too much of a step further to conclude that fat eventually makes its way to your waistline (although, to be fair, that was never said by Dr Keys).

There are many problems with the Fat Theory, starting from the very beginning. When you add the other 15 countries to Dr Keys' graph, the results are all over the place. Some countries (like Greece) have a very high-fat diet but a very low incidence of heart disease. Some countries (like Finland) have a very low-fat diet but a very high incidence of heart disease. The nice neat correlation that the theory predicts vanishes in a puff of statistical dust. Dr Keys modified his theory to accommodate these observations during the sixties. He said that what he'd meant to say was that saturated fat (largely from animals) was the problem and that unsaturated fat (largely from plants) was okay. He observed that the fat in the Greek diet comes from olive plants but the fat in the Finnish diet comes from animals and fish. This explained the graph to everyone's satisfaction. So Dr Keys and his wife decided to create a diet based on what people who live on the Mediterranean Sea eat, since they appear to have such a low incidence of heart disease. The 'Mediterranean diet' (as it is now known) lives on to the present day.

A more fundamental problem with the Fat Theory is that no one could replicate the results. The theory says that if you give people a high-fat diet, they will get fat. That was easy enough to do as long as the fat came with a load of sugar (think doughnuts). But if the sugar was eliminated, feeding lab rats high-fat diets did not make them fat. And even though you're not allowed to do this kind of thing to humans in labs, there are a few indigenous populations that do quite nicely on extremely high-fat diets. The Masai people of Kenya (who apparently hold similar views to my children when it comes to vegetables) live on nothing but beef cattle, and even go so far as to drink only milk and blood (for feasts). The North American Inuits (Eskimos, to the less politically correct) subsist on a diet consisting almost entirely of whale blubber.

An important note is that fat most definitely will make you fat if you still have fructose in your diet. With your appetite control system stuck at 'eat as much as you want', then eating fat is the most efficient way to pile on the kilos (because gram for gram it contains nearly twice the calories of carbohydrates or proteins). However, once fructose is eliminated and you complete your withdrawal, then there is no need to concern yourself with the fat content of foods. In fact, you'll be better off if you eat full-fat foods rather than their low-fat siblings.

Low-fat foods

Low-fat foods are engineered to taste approximately the same as the full-fat version. The most common way of achieving this is to increase the sugar content, and then to increase the salt content to balance the additional sweetness. The result isn't exactly the same as the original because you lose some of the 'mouth-feel' that fat brings to the table, but it's pretty close. For someone who wants to stop being a sugarholic, this means that low-fat foods are generally off the shopping list because the last thing you want is to be buying foods with extra sugar added. But there's an even more compelling reason to avoid low-fat foods.

Cholesterol

Contrary to popular belief, there is only one kind of cholesterol. There is no good, bad or even ugly cholesterol; there's just cholesterol. Cholesterol is a fat and is therefore not soluble in water. Since our blood is a water-based solution, this presents a bit of a problem in the logistics department. Cholesterol needs to be transported from the liver (where it is made) to the places where it is needed (pretty much everywhere in the body – it's used to make cell membranes). So, the body packages the cholesterol with some proteins (called lipoproteins) in a bundle of molecules ready for shipping.

HDL and LDL cholesterol

Lipoproteins are the transport system (like an empty semitrailer) for cholesterol (and other fats). When lipoproteins are in the bloodstream (on the highway), they are referred to as HDL cholesterol ('good' cholesterol) or LDL cholesterol ('bad' cholesterol). The goodness or badness of the cholesterol depends entirely on the size of the transport. Goods (cholesterol) transported on small trucks (HDL) are not bad, but goods transported on big trucks (LDL) are bad.

There are five major groups of lipoproteins but I want to focus on the group that doctors sometimes call 'bad' cholesterol. Lipoproteins are grouped by size. Low Density Lipoproteins or LDL particles are loosely packed (hence 'low density') and, as a result, relatively large. LDL particles transport cholesterol manufactured in the liver out to the cells. When a doctor says you have a 'bad' cholesterol reading, she is talking about LDL being outside a target range (2.6 to 3.3 mmol/L). If you get too far out of that range (greater than 6.5 mmol/L), there is a good chance you will be prescribed a class of drugs called statins to lower your LDL cholesterol levels.

LDL particles, although relatively large, come in a range of sizes. People can be divided into two main groups according to which size is most common in their bodies. Some people have mostly large LDL particles and some people have mostly small ones. The folks with predominantly large particles are called pattern A, and the others, pattern B. Whether you are pattern A (large) or pattern B (small) is pretty much a matter of genetics. If both your parents are pattern A, then you are more likely to be pattern A, and so on. Which pattern you are matters because if you are predominantly pattern A, your LDL reading is not an indicator of the risk of heart disease. You are likely to be told by your doctor that you have a high LDL reading, but because you are pattern A (and unfortunately the blood test won't show which pattern you are), then you are unlikely to be at risk. But pattern B people are at considerable risk. The small size of the pattern B–LDL particles means that they are more easily embedded in the walls of blood vessels and this ultimately leads to the development of blockages.

In June 2000, Dr Krauss and his team at the Lawrence Berkeley National Laboratory, Department of Molecular Medicine at the University of California, published some very interesting results on experiments they had been doing on low-fat diets. What they found was that if you put a pattern A person on an extremely low-fat diet (where less than 25 per cent of the calories come from fat; the Pritikin Diet for example, is 10–15 per cent fat), they change to pattern B. So, the study showed that if you put some people on a low-fat diet, you increased their risk of heart disease. This happened because the change in diet caused them to convert from pattern A–LDL (large) to pattern B–LDL (small) particles.

As far as I can tell, Dr Krauss wasn't concerned what else was in the diet, just that it was low in fat. When someone goes on a low-fat diet, their carbohydrate intake generally increases. So, maybe Dr Krauss's low-fat diet was destructive not because of the fat itself but because the diet was high-carbohydrate (and therefore high-fructose, in our modern society). A more recent study involving 74 Swiss primary-school children has revealed that the more fructose a child eats, the smaller their LDL particle size is likely to be. In other words, a child on a high-fructose diet is likely to have small (pattern B) LDL particles and a child on a low-fructose diet is not.

There's a double whammy in all this. As I've mentioned, most low-fat foods in the supermarket are higher in fructose than their full-fat equivalents. So, whether it is the low-fat or the high-fructose part of the diet that is causing the LDL particles to shrink, foods low in fat and high in fructose are probably not a good idea. Unfortunately, there are no cheap and easy tests for LDL particle size. But if the Swiss study is to be believed, maybe you don't need to know. If the amount of fructose in your diet largely determines your LDL particle size, maybe all you need to know is that you can significantly reduce your risk of heart disease by not eating fructose.

Quite a few readers of Sweet Poison *have posted the results of their blood tests on the Sweet Poison Forum. Here are a few of the posts:*

My partner has changed his diet by switching from sugar to dextrose (six teaspoons per day in coffee) and cutting out fruitcake completely. His cholesterol (down from 3.2 to 2.7) and triglycerides (down from 1.3 to 0.6) are the lowest they have been in three years. He is 5 foot 10 inchs and 72 kilos. He is eating more now, just to maintain weight – pretty good, I think, at age 49. My triglycerides have dropped from 1.2 to 0.9 and I am ecstatic!

Koboli

Just got my results – these based on six months of cutting out sugar but increasing cheese, spreads, and even eating pies and chips. I have never eaten fried or fatty foods but have always consumed a lot of sugar!

Cholesterol *was* 6.9 *now* 6.0 (recommended less than 5.5)

Triglyceride *was* 2.3 *now* 1.3 (recommended less than 2.0)

HDL ('good' cholesterol) *was* 1.3 *now* 1.5 (recommended above 1.1)

LDL ('bad' cholesterol) *was* 4.6 *now* 3.9 (recommended less than 2.5)

Coronary risk *was* 5.3 *now* 4.0 (recommended less than 4)

Vicki J

I was impressed with the results after just one month off fructose. My triglyceride has halved from the previous test a year ago, from 2.6 to 1.3 (recommended less than 1.5). My HDL cholesterol is up slightly (0.75 up to 1.0), to the edge of the recommended range. The triglyceride/HDL ratio, supposedly the strongest indicator of heart attack, is down from 3.5 to 1.3 (recommended less than 2). My LDL was unchanged and total cholesterol slightly up, but both in recommended range.

Mikedufty

Fat is not bad if your appetite control is working again. As a general rule, avoid foods that are engineered to be low-fat.

Rule 4: Don't concern yourself with fat content other than to steer clear of low-fat foods.

We have been brainwashed into believing that full-fat is necessarily bad, but this is not so, especially for fructophobes.

At the supermarket

Supermarkets are laid out like Las Vegas casinos. If you've ever stayed in Las Vegas, you'll know that the casinos are designed to provide you with maximum opportunities for gambling. After you check-in, you probably want to go to your room for a nice cup of tea and a lie down (after your travels). But in order to get to the lifts, you have to cross the gambling floor. If you decide to leave your room and partake of

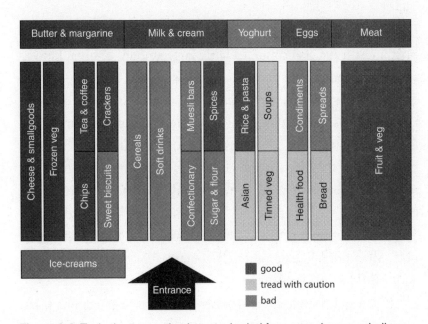

Figure 2.4: Typical supermarket layout, shaded for recovering sugarholics

a hotel meal, once again the only route is across the gambling floor. Supermarkets operate on the same principle. Between the entrance and most of the things a shopper is likely to buy every day lie aisles of sugar-filled delights. I've drawn a plan of the food bits of my local supermarket; yours is probably much the same.

A quick look at the plan will show you that shopping the perimeter is not a bad strategy for a recovering sugarholic. After you give up sugar, there are whole aisles that no longer require your attention. Shopping trips suddenly become a lot shorter when you can skip half the supermarket.

What to buy
Fruits

Whole fruits (and, to a much lesser extent, vegetables) do contain fructose – in some cases, very large amounts. But I've labelled the fruit section safe for sugarholics for two reasons.

Fibre

First, most fruits also contain a fairly large amount of fibre. Fibre is a type of carbohydrate present in most foods that naturally contain carbohydrates, but we can't completely digest it. A very common type of fibre is the cellulose that forms the cell walls of plants. This is the hard stringy bits of plants that provide structure. Cows love fibre because they have a special extra stomach full of fibre-eating bacteria. Unfortunately, our extra tummy was left on the drawing board, so we can eat fibre but have a limited ability to digest it. There are two types of fibre: soluble (dissolves in water) and insoluble. Most fibre-containing foods contain about one-third soluble and two-thirds insoluble fibre.

If you put soluble fibre in water, it turns to a gelatinous mass, whereas insoluble fibre just sits there like a woodchip at the bottom of the glass. (Wood is largely insoluble fibre. You could eat it but it would pass straight through your gut unchanged. You'll be familiar with the concept if you have ever eaten watermelon seeds and then inspected the, ah, results.) Insoluble fibre behaves like drain cleaner in that it keeps things moving along in the gut. It also adds bulk to the food that contains it, making us feel physically fuller when we eat it.

Soluble fibre is significantly less easy to understand. We have no innate ability to digest soluble fibre either, but we do have billions of little passengers who can help us out. Bacteria in our colon (large intestine) can do the job. These little chaps happily munch away and turn soluble fibre into fats, waste and energy. So, a large proportion of soluble fibre ends up in our bloodstream as fat. Today, food manufacturers are boosting the apparent fibre content of foods by adding soluble fibre such as inulin, wheat dextrin and polydextrose (see box, page 187). While 'fibre' looks good on the label, it's effectively another word for 'fat', in this case.

But not all soluble fibres are equal. Bacteria produce three primary fats from soluble fibre – butyrate, propionate and acetate – in different amounts. Most fruits and vegetables produce them in the ratio of 20% butyrate: 20% propionate: 60% acetate. As far as the bacteria are concerned, the only real point to the exercise is to produce large amounts of butyrate, which is what they use for energy; propionate and acetate are just by-products that enter our bloodstream and are used by our livers almost immediately. And this is where the story gets a little uncertain.

For a few decades, researchers have known that if you give people a high-fibre diet, good things happen around their blood sugar and insulin control. All sorts of theories have been put forward, but it is still far from clear why. What is abundantly evident is that fibre intake reduces the damage done by fructose intake.

Fructose encourages the liver to produce fat, stimulates our hunger and dulls our appetite control. Fibre seems to work in reverse, but we're not sure how. All that science leads us to the blindingly obvious conclusion that we have evolved an ability to eat small amounts of fructose as long as it comes in its original fibre packaging, like a piece of fruit (with skin). But the science also suggests that some level of innate soluble fibre helps our bodies mitigate fructose damage, while added soluble fibre is not so desirable.

Fructose concentrate

The second feature of fruit that makes it safe for sugarholics is that it contains a lot of water, which gives it bulk. That bulk significantly affects how much fructose you can take in from the fruit. You would need to juice three to four large apples to produce the juice in a small (250 ml) glass of juice. A child will easily drink a small glass of juice alongside a full meal. But try giving them four large apples and then expecting them to eat anything else. The juice and the apples contain the same amount of fructose but one is a meal and one is an insignificant add-on to a meal. Fruit juice is pure sugar and water with some vitamin C thrown in. But the fruit it comes from contains the fibre antidote to the fructose poison that it contains.

The same goes for dried fruit (or congealed fruit juice, as I prefer to call it). Drying the fruit has the same effect as juicing it: it concentrates the sugar and eliminates the bulk. With dried fruit, the fibre is still present, but the lack of bulk enables you to consume significantly larger quantities than if you were eating the whole fruit. A small box (40 g) of sultanas contains all the sugar of about 130 grapes (approximately one kilogram). You shouldn't eat either in one sitting, but it is very easy to do with the handful of sultanas contained in the box.

How much fruit?

The fibre in fruit keeps the fructose under control in the small quantities found in one or two pieces of whole fruit, but this is not an excuse for eating vast quantities of fruit. Some of the most recent fibre research suggests that what is eaten with the fibre matters a lot. Soluble fibre eaten as part of whole grains drags through some of the starch for digestion as if it were fibre, but the effect is far less significant with fibre eaten as part of fruit. By increasing the proportion of fruit in your diet, you eliminate some of the other more starchy sources of carbohydrate, and reduce the overall beneficial effect of the fibre.

Which fruit?

Neither is all fruit created equal. A recovering sugarholic wants fruit that is low in fructose and high in fibre, but some of the most popular fruits are just the opposite.

Figure 2.5 (page 108) shows a selection of fruits you're likely to find in the local supermarket. It plots each fruit's fibre content against its fructose content. The further towards the top left corner of the graph (high fructose, low fibre) a fruit lies, the less desirable it is. Fruits in the bottom right corner (low fructose, high fibre) are the best choice.

The best way to use this graph is to notice the relative positions of each fruit rather than being overly precise about the exact values. The amount of fructose in a fruit changes from species to species. So, for example, some types of apple are much sweeter than others. Since the sweetness comes largely from fructose, this means that sweeter apples are higher in fructose. How ripe a piece of fruit is also changes the fructose content. As fruit ripens, it converts glucose to fructose. That's why ripe bananas taste sweeter than unripe ones. In the graph, I have used average amounts of fructose for each fruit type just to give an idea of their relative positions.

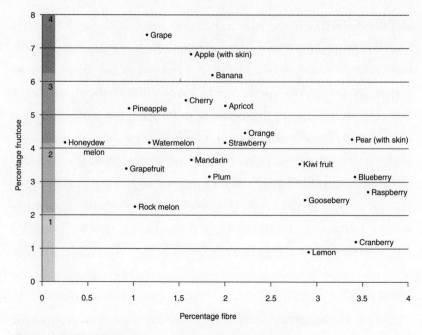

Figure 2.5: Fibre and fructose content of popular fruits

The fructose values in the chart have been calculated by adding half the sucrose value to the whole fructose value using standard databases of fruit-sugar content. That way, the fructose half of the sucrose is also accurately included in the calculation. A small banana (with skin) or a large banana (without skin) weighs 100 g, and a medium apple (with skin) is also around the 100 g mark. So, I've chosen 100 g as the standard serve for this graph. The shaded bar up the left side shows how many teaspoons of table sugar would be required to deliver the same amount of fructose found in a 100 g serve of the fruit. At a glance, you can see that 100 g of watermelon will serve up the equivalent of two teaspoons of sugar and a banana sends about three teaspoons your way.

Fibre content varies significantly between fruits. So, even though a pear has the same amount of fructose as an orange, it is a better choice because it has almost twice the fibre. Berries clearly win the day, with cranberries, raspberries, gooseberries and blueberries all scoring well. The best fruit is the lemon (surprise, surprise!), but for those who prefer something a little more edible, kiwi fruits and pears are good choices. At the other end of the scale, grapes are to be avoided and caution needs to be exercised around apples, bananas, cherries, pineapples and apricots. Now you know why apple and grape puree is the filler of choice for a large proportion of fruit-based snacks. The manufacturers can claim these products have 'no added sugar' while they're actually serving up something very high in sugar (especially when pureed).

The subject of fruit is complex and less than clear even to nutritionists, but there are some very simple commonsense messages we can take away.

1. **Fruit should be treated with caution and not consumed in large quantities** (no more than two pieces per day for an adult or one for a child). We are encouraged by various health authorities to eat two pieces of fruit and five vegetables per day. Many people think those numbers are mix-and-match, i.e. that you can make up for a lack of vegies in your diet by eating extra fruit. However, the science suggests that we should be treating two pieces of fruit as an absolute maximum (and that dried fruit and juice should not be classed as 'fruit' at all).

2. **'Foods' such as dried fruit and fruit juices, which encourage us to consume large quantities of fructose, should be completely avoided.**

3. **When choosing fruit, select types that have lower fructose and higher fibre**. For example, given a choice between a slice of watermelon and an orange, go for the orange. Or even better, choose a peach, a strawberry or a mandarin (because they have more fibre).

Vegetables

There is no such thing as a bad vegetable. All vegetables contain some level of fructose, but it is insignificant and vastly overwhelmed by the fibre content. Figure 2.6 plots fructose against fibre for most of the vegetables you are likely to encounter in the supermarket. Note that the scales are not the same as the fruit graph. The vegetable with the highest fructose content (beetroot) would be in the same position as kiwi fruit (one of the lowest-fructose fruits) in Figure 2.5.

Once again, the shaded bar up the left side shows how many teaspoons of table sugar would be required to deliver the same amount of fructose found in a 100g serve of each vegetable. In terms of vegetables, 100g is approximately one small tomato (yes, I know it's not a vegetable, but you're more likely to find it in a salad than a fruit salad), one medium onion or 10 button mushrooms (and yes, I know it's a fungi . . . sheesh).

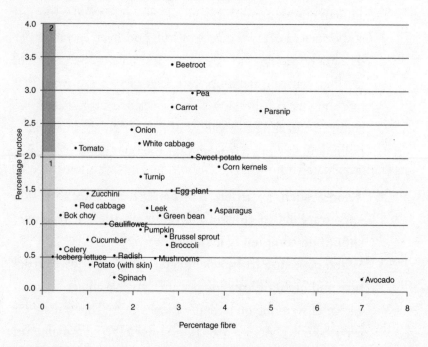

Figure 2.6: Fibre and fructose content of popular vegetables

Clearly, you can't go past an avocado on either the fruit or the vegtable graph. It has practically no fructose and a vast amount of fibre per serve. And while none of the vegetables could be described as bad for you, given the choice, it might be wise to head for broccoli, pumpkin, brussel sprouts or beans ahead of carrots or peas.

The same warnings apply to vegetable juices as fruit juices. Juicing a vegetable is no better for you than juicing a fruit, because it simply extracts all the sugar and concentrates it. While carrot juice contains only half the sugar of apple juice, there's still the equivalent of two and a half teaspoons of the stuff in a small (250 ml) glass.

On your shopping expedition, fill your basket with as much vegetable matter as you can stomach. You will get well and truly sick of it long before it makes you sick.

Nuts

You'll probably encounter nuts in the fruit and vegetable section of the supermarket, so it's worth taking a look at their sugar contents. Like vegetables, there's no such thing as a bad nut. Some have more fructose than others but even the worst of them, from a fructose perspective, have huge amounts of fibre.

An avocado is the best vegetable for fibre by a country mile, but it's nothing compared to the best of the nuts (linseeds), which have approximately four times the fibre. Linseeds, sunflower seeds, walnuts and hazelnuts are all fantastic choices in terms of fructose content. Cashews and macadamias have slightly more fructose, but you'd still need to eat 100 g (about 70 cashews or 50 macadamias) to get the same amount of fructose as in one carrot. And in the case of macadamias, you'd be getting more than twice the fibre.

Even the confectionery of the nut world, the peanut, barely rates on the fructose scale. Peanuts pack about the same punch as kiwi fruit (the lowest of the fruits) but have seven times the fibre content.

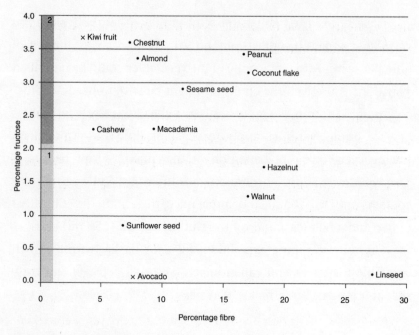

Figure 2.7: Fibre and fructose content of popular nuts

Even the relatively high-fructose nuts (almonds and chestnuts) still outgun kiwi fruit for fibre by three to one. You can't choose a bad nut but the best choices would be anything below and to the right of a cashew on the graph.

Meat

The next fructose-free area you will encounter as you circle the perimeter of your supermarket is the meat section. Nothing here will do a recovering sugarholic any harm. Meat does not contain any sugar, so knock yourself out. The only possible word of caution is around some of the fancy marinated meats. Some supermakets have started introducing prepackaged roast and other meats that have been marinaded for you. The marinade is usually very high in sugar and this type of product should generally be avoided unless you discover one low in sugar. Read the labels, and if you see anything under 'sugars', move on. Aside from that, everything is fair game (pun very much intended).

Eggs

The poor old egg has had a really bad time from the anti-fat and anti-cholesterol lobbies over the last few decades. But rest assured, there is no sugar in eggs. And once your appetite control system is back in working order, any fats they contain will be properly regulated by your body. Buy eggs at will.

Yoghurts

You will already have emptied your fridge of all but the tartest of European and natural yoghurts, so don't go filling your trolley with anything else. During the withdrawal period, you might find some of the diet varieties (sweetened with various artificial sweeteners) helpful if sweet yoghurt has been a big part of your diet up till now, but in general there is very little in this section for you (see chapter 3 for more on substitution during withdrawal). The reality in today's supermarket is that the yoghurt section is a slightly runnier version of the ice-cream section with some spurious health messages plastered on the packaging for good measure. There's no need to pause here for long.

Milk and cream

The labels on unflavoured milk and cream will say that they contain 4.7 per cent sugar. This sugar is all lactose and you can safely ignore it. Whole milk and unflavoured creams are fine in your new diet. Fill the trolley with them. I have just two cautions in this section. First, avoid reduced-fat products. As I outlined above, reduced-fat diets have been directly linked to changes in blood-fat chemistry which cause heart disease. And second, I'm sure I don't need to tell you not to buy the kind of whipped cream you spray from a can or any kind of flavoured cream or milk. But just in case, the only things it is acceptable to buy in this section are the unflavoured milks and creams. Obviously, chocolate milk has sugar added and so do the fancy sweetened creams. Anything you buy in this section must not taste sweet.

Butter and margarine

You've been told for years to seek out margarines and 'healthy fat' spreads full of all kinds of things to help stop cholesterol reabsorption (whatever that is) and reduce your risk of heart disease. Very little of this is supported by decent reseach. By 'decent' research, I mean research that adjusts for confounding factors such as what else was in the subject's diet at the time of the study. For example, you will find studies that show that eating palmitic acid increases your risk of heart disease. Palmitic acid is a saturated fatty acid found in things like butter but not some margarines. But (so far at least) the studies ignore the fact that palmitic acid is also the primary output of your liver when exposed to fructose. So, whilst the result (that palmitic acid is associated with heart disease) is likely to be correct, the real source of the majority of it has been largely ignored.

In the late 1960s, John Yudkin's team at the University of London performed an interesting experiment on 11 people. Yudkin was trying to see whether telling people to eat fewer carbohydrates made any difference to anything else they ate. The team monitored the diets of these 11 average people (they were not overweight) aged 21–51 for two weeks, to see what they normally ate. Then, for a further two weeks, they told them that they had to restrict carbohydrates to 50 g per day (essentially forcing them to eliminate all sugars, breads and grains). They were also told that they could eat as much of anything else (fat, meat, fish, milk and cheese) as they wanted. They were not to concern themselves with the calories or the fat content – they could just pig out. Their only guide as to what to eat, apart from carbohydrates, was to be their own desires.

After two weeks of this, the team found that the participants had reduced their daily calorie intake (on average) by about 25 per cent (about 1 kg worth of body fat a week for an adult male) but still felt perfectly satisfied. In fact, many of them voluntarily reported feeling more energetic and generally healthier. They did not perceive themselves as being on a diet or being in any way restricted (other than to avoid carbohydrates). Later, Yudkin tried variations of the experient where the only thing that was resticted was sugar intake and the results were similar.

It's interesting to compare these results with a similar experiment run in the forties by Ancel Keys. He recruited 36 healthy (normal weight) young men and put them on a diet that restricted fat intake with the aim of reducing total calories by 25 per cent for 24 weeks. The men were held in an encampment and their food was restricted by force. As expected, the result was significant weight loss. But as the time wore on, the men thought ceaselessly about food. They became lethargic and reported feeling cold all the time. They became depressed and developed bleeding disorders. A few developed more serious psychological disorders.

Both Yudkin's and Keys' group lost weight. But one group felt on top of the world and completely unrestricted, while the other was desperately hungry and unhealthy. The only appreciable difference between the two is that Yudkin restricted carbohydrates (and in subsequent studies narrowed it down to sugar) while Keys restricted fat consumption. One group happily consumed 25 per cent fewer calories without really trying, while the other also ate 25 per cent fewer calories but desperately craved food.

If your appetite control system is working, you will not be able to eat too much fat. The CCK will work properly and you will feel full appropriate to what you have eaten. Once your apetite control system is working, you will feel more full more quickly on fat than you will on bread, and find yourself having to make choices about what you eat based simply on how quickly you want to get full. Having that large serve of chips for afternoon tea will mean that you won't want dinner. If dinner was going to be yak's liver on toast, maybe you wouldn't mind, but if it was going to be Gran's best roast, then you might decide to skip the chips. One of the things that I have found since going fructose-free is that I am now much more easily satisfied. And once I feel full, I really don't want to eat more.

This was a strange new experience for me at the end of the withdrawal period, but now it's something I really need to be aware of. I know that my body is keeping count, so if I graze through-out the day, I literally will not be able to eat dinner. When you are addicted to sugar and your appetite control is stuck half-on, you can keep eating and eating and eating. But once you are fructose-free and your appetite control is working, it will be counting your calories for you and will stop you in your tracks if you try to eat too much. And it's a shame if that means you've got to push back from Gran's roast before you've even started on the potato.

So, the things to avoid in the butter and margarine section of the supermarket are the chemisty experiments known as 'mar-garine' and 'low-fat spread'. There is nothing wrong with full-fat butter other than the difficulty of spreading it straight out of the fridge. When you are a sugarholic, you will need to consciously moderate your fat consumption but after you start withdrawal and for the rest of your life, you can let you appetite control do the work for you.

My aim was to lose 30 kg. Well, I have lost 16 kg since I started this sugar-free walk in November 08 (it's now July 09). So only 14 kg to go. Wooo hooo.

I did go a month without losing any weight, but I didn't mind because I was giving my skin a chance to catch up with my weight loss! The month I did not lose weight was when winter kicked in. My body must have wanted to keep that layer of fat.

I live on my own and I find it hard to cook for one. So I am cooking as if I had a family and freezing meals. Also cooking soups and using more vegies than I ever used before. Sometimes I do eat fast food but notice I am not enjoying it as I used to. I also find the amount of meat that I eat has dropped significantly.

Marita

Cheese and smallgoods

There is not much danger lurking in the shelves in this section. Cheese will have sugar on the label but it is all lactose, so there's no need for concern. The only real concern will probably be the flavoured versions of things like cottage cheese and cream cheese. 'Flavoured' is usually just another word for 'sugar added'. Cured meats and smallgoods are generally sugar-free but if in doubt, check the label. If you see any sugar listed, then it has been added and you should avoid the product. Meat does not contain sugar of any kind.

Bread

Now that you have successfully circumnavigated the supermarket, there's really not much need to venture into the interior rows. The only exception to this (at least in my supermarket)

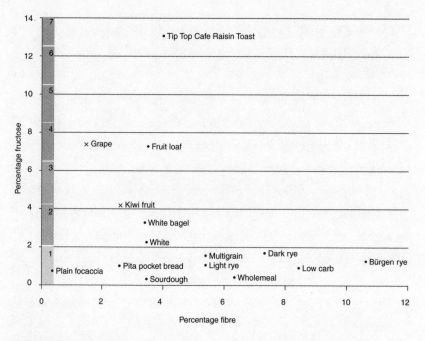

Figure 2.8: Fibre and fructose content of popular brands of bread

is for bread. Most bread is relatively low in sugar but some is surprisingly high.

All breads contain some sugar. All of the standard unflavoured white breads (the worst of a good bunch, with the highest sugar and lower fibre) lie somewhere between 0.5 and 4 per cent sugar (2 per cent fructose). This is about half the best fruit (kiwi fruit) and with equivalent amounts of fibre. Multigrain and brown (whole-meal and rye) breads are also low-sugar and have approximately twice as much fibre. Bagels should be avoided as a regular part of the diet because they contain, on average, twice the sugar of equivalent bread. A white bagel, for example, has 6.5 g of sugar per 100 g compared to 4 g for equivalent white bread. In terms of sugar and fibre content, a white bagel is nearly identical to the average kiwi fruit. If you like your bread white but would rather not have the sugar at all, then sourdough (as the name implies) is the way to go. 'Low-carb, high-fibre' breads might seem tempting, but the way they obtain their enviable postion on the graph is by substituting some of the sugar in white bread with inulin. Inulin is a man-made fibre which some of the most up-to-date research suggests bypasses your appetite control system in a different (but just as effective) way as fructose. I explain this in chapter 4 (see page 185), but for now, I'd be leaving it off the shopping list.

There is no good reason to eat any kind of fruit loaf or raisin toast. A standard serve (90–100 g) contains between four and seven teaspoons of sugar. The Tip Top Cafe Raisin Toast is the highest-sugar loaf I have encountered, at just over 13 per cent fructose (26 per cent sugar), largely because it has a very generous serve of raisins in every slice. The thing to remember about bread is that most people eat a lot of it during the day. By the time you've had two slices of toast with breakfast and four slices with lunch, you are up around 300 g of daily intake. If the bread is a standard white bread, that could mean around 6 g of fructose (the equivalent of three teaspoons of sugar) per day from bread alone. If you are a big bread eater, go for the sourdough (white) or the lowest-sugar rye or multigrain you can find. My personal favourite is Bürgen Rye, which I like toasted with butter and Vegemite.

Spreads

Nestled near the breads in most supermarkets, you'll find things to spread on it (who says shopkeepers aren't smart?). There is almost nothing worth buying from this section of the supermarket and the recovering sugarholic should avert their eyes as they pass through here on the way to the perimeter. But just for fun, I've listed the average sugar contents of the types of things you are likely to find in the spreads section.

Spread	% sugar
Honey	82
Fruit jams and conserves	65
Hazelnut spreads	55
Low-sugar jams and conserves	30–40
Peanut butter with honey	20
Peanut butter	9
Peanut butter without added salt	5.5
Cream cheese spread	2.1
Vegemite	1.4

Vegemite is (thankfully!) an acceptable spread. One 20 g serve contains about 0.28 g of sugar (0.14 g of fructose), which is well within your daily limit. If you're not a fan of Australia's national dish, then peanut butter without added salt is worth considering. When they don't add salt to peanut butter, they also leave the sugar on the shelf. Each 20 g serve contains about 0.55 g of fructose, so you'd need to eat four serves just to get the equivalent of a spoonful of sugar. Cream cheese spread is also an option. The 2.1 per cent sugar is all lactose, so it is effectively 0 per cent fructose.

All 'mites are not the same. Some people are not fans of Vegemite (hard to believe, I know). People of English or New Zealand heritage often prefer the taste of Marmite or Promite. But there are some very sugary reasons to avoid both of these alternatives.

'mite spread	% sugar
Kraft Vegemite	1.4
Sanitarium Marmite	11.8
Masterfoods Promite	18.4

Everything else on the list should be a no-go zone for you. Honey is often sold as the 'natural alternative' (although it's not clear what it's an alternative to). But it doesn't matter if honey has been hand-farmed by your neighbour's grandad, it's still likely to be in the 80 per cent range for total sugars (and 40 per cent for fructose). Jams and conserves are also chock-full of sugar and must be avoided. And no matter how many ads you see testifying to their health benefits, chocolate hazelnut spreads are simply spreadable chocolate bars.

If Vegemite, peanut butter without salt or cream cheese spread don't appeal, try one of my kids' favourites: avocado. Fresh avocado smeared on toast is a delicious spread, and you can liven it up with a little salt, pepper and maybe even a squeeze of lemon. Avocado scores off the scale on the vegetable chart (above), being very high in fibre and having almost no fructose. As spreads go, it doesn't come any better than avocado.

Condiments

Condiments (and by that I mean sauces and flavours designed to be added to food after it is served) are very dangerous territory for the recovering sugarholic. There is more sugar in barbecue sauce (55 per cent) than there is in chocolate topping (43 per cent). The reason barbecue sauce doesn't taste as sweet is that it is also loaded with salt to balance out the sweet taste.

Sauce	% sugar
Barbecue	48–55
Hoi sin	25–50
Steak	45
Sweet chilli	43–49
Brown (for example, HP)	26
Ketchup	25
Tomato	21–36
Worcestershire	15–36
Apple	15
Tartare	6–10
Laksa	5–10
Fish	6
Taco	1.5
Soy	1
Tabasco	0

Some sauces range considerably in sugar content between brands. It's always worth looking at the label on your favourite brand and comparing it to others. Worcestershire sauce is a great example of the kind of variation you can get. Holbrooks is only 14.7 per cent sugar and Lea & Perrins is 16.9 per cent. But Masterfoods is 35.9 per cent – more than twice as much as Holbrooks. Similarly, most tomato sauces are in the range 21–25 per cent sugar, but Wool-worths Select brand is 36 per cent, putting it within reach of some of the lower-sugar barbecue sauces. By the look of the list above, you're going to need to develop a taste for taco sauce, soy sauce or Tabasco, or learn to live without sauce. There are very few good sauces, which is perhaps why children (and men in blue singlets on meat pie commercials) like everything drowned in litres of sauce.

At all costs, avoid reduced-fat sauces. They usually contain around twice the sugar of the regular equivalent. Traditional tartare, for example, is around the 10 per cent mark, but reduced-fat tartare is typically in the range 20–22 per cent. You can, of course, make your own tomato sauce by simply diluting tomato paste. (The paste is usually around 11 per cent sugar in the concentrated tub, but considerably less once diluted, depending on how much water you add). You can also just add dextrose to passata (be careful of the brand – some add sugar) or make the rather complex but delicious recipe for ketchup that appears in the recipe section.

If relish or chutney is your thing, then I have some bad news for you. They should be in the confectionery section of the super-market (with the sauces).

Chutney/Relish	% sugar
Fruit chutney	29–39
Gherkin relish	31
Barbecue relish	24
Tomato chutney or relish	18
Corn relish	17
Salsa	7–9
Pesto	2–5

For some reason, this sort of condiment excites the creative bones in the food manufacturers, and the particular flavours and constitutions of each chutney or relish change quite frequently. So, if you are just ducking quickly (and I mean quickly!) into the condiments section for a pesto, check the label first. If you see more than 5 per cent sugar, put it back and move on.

The other major inhabitants of the condiment section are mustards, mayonnaises and salad dressings. The news on mustards is all good. The average mustard has no sugar, or just a teeny bit if it is a wholegrain variety (around 2 per cent from the grains). Mayonnaises divide neatly into two camps: the stuff you have previously been told not to eat (whole-egg mayonnaise) because it contains the dreaded eggs, and the stuff I am going to tell you not to eat now (the rest). Whole-egg mayonnaise is very low in sugar (most brands are less than 2 per cent and quite a few are zero). If you're a mayo fan, fill the trolley with these. There is only one you need to watch out for: Praise makes a reduced-fat whole-egg mayo that is 13 per cent sugar. The other kind of mayonnaise is the non-egg-based stuff marketed as 'traditional mayonnaise'. The full-fat versions of these are around the 8.5 per cent sugar mark and the reduced-fat versions are up to 21 per cent sugar, so avoid them at all costs.

Unfortunately, traditional mayo is used as the basis for commercial coleslaw, so you can expect a big serve of sugar if you buy pre-made coleslaw from the supermarket. Besides, making your own with the kids is good fun – seriously! (See page 204 for a recipe. Mixing in the mayo is best done with the hands, which is where the kids come in.) I defy you or your sugar-munching friends to detect the difference between this coleslaw and the sugar-loaded variety, and it is almost (except for the carrot and cabbage) sugar-free.

Salad dressings don't exactly qualify for confectionery status, but some are alarmingly high in sugar and most of them should be avoided.

Salad dressing	% sugar
Thousand island fat-free	19
Thousand island	17
Balsamic vinegar	15
French fat-free	9–17
French	7–13
Italian or Caesar fat-free	10
Italian or Caesar	5
Ranch	6
Lemon juice	2.5
Vinegar	0
Olive oil	0

You might be surprised to find that balsamic vinegar has so much sugar. The reason for the difference between it and vinegar is that balsamic vinegar is not actually vinegar at all. In fact, it is a reduction of the syrup of sweet wine grapes. True vinegar is made by further fermenting wine (the word 'vinegar' derives from the Old French *vin aigre*, which means 'sour wine'). In balsamic, all the grape sugar is still there, but in vinegar, it's all been fermented (initially to ethanol in the wine and ultimately to acetic acid).

The best thing to put on salad is air. If that's not to your taste, try combining some or all of the last three things on the list above with some chopped herbs; the result should do the trick and is virtually sugar-free.

Why bother?

Step 5 is about creating a sugar-free oasis in your home. If you follow the guidelines laid out in this section, nothing in your kitchen or fridge will contain a significant amount of sugar. It's impossible to snack on sugar if there is none available. It's impossible to accidentally throw together a high-sugar meal if every ingredient in your kitchen is certified (by you) sugar-free. I know it looks like a complex analysis of the weekly shop, and it is, the first time you do it. But after a few weeks, you will become used to re-stocking from the same relatively limited sections. Your shopping time will decrease. Your shopping bill will decrease (all that packaged food costs a motza). And your sugar-free kitchen will be preserved automatically, simply because you will be in the habit of shopping this way.

3. MEAL PLANNER

Eliminating sugar from your diet isn't as hard as it sounds. You will never reduce it to zero (unless you stop eating altogether, but then you won't be worrying about much except whether the funeral plot has flowers or not). Now that you know how to safely navigate the supermarket, here are some suggestions for sugar-free meals (or as close as it's possible to get). One thing you'll notice about these meals is that I don't suggest portion sizes or ask you to count calories. Your appetite control will start to return to normal as you progress through the withdrawal period. This means that meals you would have polished off easily before will now be impossible to finish. Your body will be counting calories the way it is meant to, so there's no need for you to count too. Eat until you start to feel full or you finish the portion size you're used to, whichever comes first.

The other thing to pay attention to is hunger. I don't mean the vague, unpleasant, hunger-like irritation you have during the withdrawal period. I mean the genuine, tummy-gurgling hunger you will begin to feel after you've completed withdrawal. When you feel that hunger then you should, of course, eat; but try to avoid eating when you don't feel hungry. This may involve skipping meals altogether (only do this if you genuinely don't feel hungry) or just taking smaller portions. If you haven't started withdrawal yet, you'll have no idea what I'm talking about, but believe me, after withdrawal your appetite will be significantly diminished. This does not mean you will enjoy food less; on the contrary, because the sugar fog has lifted from your tastebuds, you will experience an intensity of flavours that you never knew existed. I found I suddenly understood what the wine tossers ('scuse French) had been going on about all this time. I could really taste a difference between cab sav and shiraz! (Before, it had all just tasted like red wine.) When you are sugar-free, your tastebuds will discover much more about food than whether it is sweet or not. However, you can't rely on your appetite to tell you how much to eat at the beginning of the withdrawal period because at that point you will feel (vaguely) hungry most of the time.

This meal planner is not the kind you're likely to find in a diet book. You won't need to search the deli for Moldavian sheep bladders for Tuesday evening's supper. Nor will you have to spend half your life finely dicing mushrooms from the south side of the hill for Wednesday's Nepalese garden salad. This meal planner is about giving you ideas for easy sugar-free meals.

An important note about dextrose monohydrate

Throughout this meal planner and the recipes that follow, I'll refer to dextrose. I'm talking about a white powder that looks like caster sugar. It is pure glucose (the good half of sugar) bonded to a water molecule. You can buy it in the home-brew section of your supermarket in 1 kg bags (usually around $3). Often dextrose can be substituted for sugar, but not always (the water molecule gives it some different properties when cooked).

At the start of the withdrawal phase, dextrose will not taste at all sweet to you. In fact, it will taste vaguely like flour with a little tingle on the tongue. Compared to sugar, dextrose is extraordinarily bland. Your tastebuds have spent the whole of your life getting used to sweetness turned up to the volume provided by sugar-laced foods, and dextrose won't cut it for them at the start of withdrawal. You will, however, notice that as you go more and more days without sugar, your tastebuds adjust. Things that never tasted particularly sweet before will start to taste sweet. I remember how bananas tasted to me when I was a sugarholic: they were a bland, uninteresting fruit that I wouldn't cross the kitchen (let alone the road) to eat. Now, they are one of the sweetest things I eat – and they really do taste extraordinarily sweet to me. Dextrose is the same. At the start of withdrawal, it will be practically tasteless, but by the end, it will taste roughly the way you remember caster sugar tasting.

The glucose warning from page 64 applies to dextrose:

Do not eat foods sweetened with dextrose (glucose) until you have completed withdrawal from sugar.

If you have not commenced withdrawal, your arteries are still laden with the output of your fructose-soaked diet. Glucose will simply spike your blood sugar levels and push up your insulin production. Neither of these things is good for you.

Breakfast

Breakfast out of a packet usually involves large quantities of sugar. Sometimes the sugar comes packaged as dried fruit but it is nonetheless sugar. The cereals chart on page 71 shows just how few cereals can be eaten safely by the recovering sugarholic. But there are a few.

Cereals

Rolled oats (that's porridge, to those of us with Scottish heritage) – if it's winter, why would you go past them? Dump some in a bowl with water or milk and shove them in the microwave for an instant, hot, sugar-free breakfast. Obviously you will not be adding any sugar or honey to your porridge, but if you are partial to a little zing, sprinkle some dextrose powder over it. Dextrose won't taste like sugar, but it will taste sweeter and sweeter the further you are from being a sugarholic. You could also cut up half a banana and mix it in. Sure, the banana contains fructose, but you are eating it in its original fibre packaging, and throwing in a bunch more fibre (in the oats) for good measure. If you prefer honey, try glucose syrup. It's a clear liquid available in the cookery section of most supermarkets. Like dextrose, glucose syrup won't taste particularly sweet when you first have it, but it grows on you as your tastebuds adjust. If you are partial to honey, then at least glucose syrup has approximately the same consistency and can be poured onto your porridge in roughly the same manner.

Weet-Bix or Vita Brits (or their generic equivalents) are good cereal choices. Once again, add dextrose powder if you want to simulate sugar, or just eat them dry with a nice layer of butter spread on top (my favourite). Shredded wheat is also a good choice, but only if you get the unflavoured variety (the flavoured ones are full of sugar).

Amongst the muesli varieties available, only Carman's Original Fruit-Free is good enough for the recovering sugarholic, and even it is borderline unacceptable at 6.6 per cent sugar (largely from some added glucose and honey, and a tiny little bit from the nuts). The rest include dried fruit, and some add honey and sugar as well.

If you are a DIY kind of person, then of course you can make your own muesli. Just make sure you use plenty of nuts from the lower right of Figure 2.7 (see page 112) and plenty of oats. Don't add dried fruit, sugar or honey but feel free to use glucose syrup or dextrose. I've included the Phillips Family Muesli recipe in chapter 5.

Toast

Choose the right bread (see pages 117–19) and toast can be a quick and easy breakfast that is virtually sugar-free. The trick is finding something low enough in sugar to spread on it. Butter is fine and some people go with plain old buttered toast. My personal favourite is Vegemite, but I was born and raised in Australia, so I have the gene. If Vegemite is not your kettle of yeast, then you can go for peanut butter without added salt (see page 120). Cream cheese spreads are a sugar-free favourite for one of my daughters, and one of my sons loves an avocado mashed up and spread on multigrain toast with a little salt, pepper and lemon juice. (This last one is a particularly good choice – it's extremely low in sugar and very high in fibre.)

You can, of course, go all fancy with toast and brew up a bruschetta with fresh tomato, capers and onion, and that would be perfectly acceptable too. Use the spreads, fruits and breads guides in chapter 2 and you won't go wrong.

Continental breakfasts

I lived in Germany for a year during my youth and it gave me quite a taste for the European continental breakfast. Unfortunately, in Australia, leaving cheeses, meats and so on in the fridge (to avoid the nasty diseases you risk if you leave them out) causes them to go rock-hard. This means that continental breakfasts in Australia are not always ideal. But, where feasible, a continental breakfast has the advantage of being almost completely sugar-free (as long as you avoid the pastries and jams) as well as being the cheapest option on a hotel menu. Most European breads are ryes or sourdoughs and are generally baked with no or very little sugar. The meat has no sugar, and the only sugar in the cheese is lactose. Avoid sweetened yoghurts and sweetened spreads, and you have a great sugar-free breakfast. You could even go fully German and throw in a boiled egg on Sundays. Or spice things up every now and then with a sliced pear or kiwi fruit.

Hot breakfasts

Hot breakfasts are perfect for the recovering sugarholic. The only things you need to watch out for are the condiments and, depending on your habits, some of the breads.

You can have eggs any way you want them: boiled, fried, poached or scrambled. You can have them as part of bacon and eggs or steak and eggs or sausage and eggs . . . (I'm sure you get the idea). The only change you might need to face is that tomato sauce is not allowed. You could try frying up a fresh tomato with the eggs to get a tomato kick. Or you could whip up a hollandaise sauce instead (see recipe in chapter 5). Another nice addition to the plate is avocado – there's something fantastic about the taste of crisp bacon and fresh avocado. And the avocado gives you a lovely big serve of fibre with your (otherwise fibre-free) breakfast.

Shop-bought pancake mixes are out. Even though they vary significantly in their sugar contents (from 8 to well over 20 per cent), they are all too high for the recovering sugarholic. But, luckily for pancake fans, I've included a recipe for pancakes made using dextrose (see chapter 5). These will initially taste a little less sweet than you are used to, but by the time you are sugar-free, you'll consider them perfectly normal. Pancakes aren't much fun on their own, but you are going to have to leave the maple syrup alone. Butter, melting slowly over a hot pancake, is a treat all on its own, but all I can offer on the syrup front is glucose syrup. Unfortunately, glucose syrup has the thicker consistency of honey rather than the runny maple-syrup-like flow, so it might not be too satisfying. You could try some fresh strawberries and perhaps sprinkle a little dextrose over the top.

Things to have for breakfast at home:

- Unflavoured rolled oats (porridge) with full-cream milk
- Weet-Bix, Vita Brits or shredded wheat (unflavoured)
- Toast with butter, Vegemite, cream cheese, peanut butter without added salt or avocado
- Eggs and bacon, sausages, hash browns, tomato or steak (or the lot)
- Dextrose pancakes (see page 243) with fresh strawberries

Drinks

As you already know, juice of any description is out. (Soft drink is too, but you're more likely to be reaching for the juice at breakfast.) The only sugar-free drinks you're likely to want at breakfast are milk (full-fat and unflavoured), water, and tea or coffee (without sugar). If you've been used to having sugar in your tea or coffee, switch to dextrose – or, if that doesn't have enough kick, use one of the artificial sweeteners such as aspartame or sucralose. If you plan to do that, take a look at chapter 4 first to make sure you are not being suckered by a sweetener (such as sorbitol) that has the same health effects as sugar. I never had sugar in my tea, but most people who did tell me that dextrose is an acceptable alternative while they get unhooked from sugar. After they are sugar-free, they usually don't bother with anything at all.

Personally, I like nothing better than a nice big glass of ice-cold, full-cream milk with my Vegemite toast for breakfast. If you've been drinking low-fat milk your whole life and can't stomach the idea of full-fat, I'd advise you to try (given the research on the damage low-fat products could be doing to your LDL cholesterol count) or else switch to water with your breakfast. (Given the quantity you use in your tea of coffee, it doesn't much matter what kind of milk you use there.)

Breakfast on the town

You don't get much more variety for breakfast when you're eating out than when you're at home. Observe these rules when ordering and you should be fine:

- No juice (not even if it's included for free – if it's delivered anyway, ask them to swap it for water or milk so you aren't tempted)
- No pastries except a plain croissant (with butter if you like)
- No cereals except oats and unflavoured Bix, Brits or shredded wheat
- Don't add sugar to anything
- No jams or honey as spreads
- No fruit toast
- No pancakes (or maple syrup, in case you were thinking of drinking it without the pancakes)
- As much bacon, eggs, hash browns, toast, butter, tomatoes, mushrooms, steak and sausages as you like
- As much water, milk, tea and coffee as you want

If you're feeling flush, you might even darken the door of your local fast-food joint for brekkie. McDonald's is the only Australian outfit that publishes a comprehensive listing of the sugar content of their foods, but it is probably representative of most fast-food outlets. Here's an analysis of their breakfast options.

McDonald's breakfast item	% sugar	Sugar (tsp)*
Hash Brown	0.0	0.00
Vegemite	1.7	0.00
All coffee- and tea-based drinks	0.0	0.00
Whipped Butter (adjusted for lactose)	0.0	0.00
Peanut Butter English Muffin Sausage McMuffin Sausage & Egg McMuffin	8.1 2.0 1.3 1.0	0.25
Bacon & Egg McMuffin	1.4	0.50
Marmalade Strawberry Jam	65.2	2.25
Deli-choices Roll – Deluxe English Muffin & Jam	4.4 14.6	2.50
Honey	82.1	2.75
Deli-choices Roll – Bacon & Egg	6.0	3.25
Plain Hotcakes	9.4	3.50
Uncle Toby's Yoghurt & Muesli Cup (adjusted for lactose)	10.5	5.00
Hotcake Syrup	53.3	7.50
Hotcakes with Syrup and Butter	20.8	11.00

*In all of the McDonald's tables, sugar quantities are rounded to the nearest quarter-teaspoon.

Because some of these items come in very small servings, I've also included an indication of how many teaspoons of sugar you will get in one serving of the product. Anything involving a hotcake, jam or cereal is not for you, but there are some other perfectly acceptable low-sugar options on the list (including my favourite, the Bacon

& Egg McMuffin). The reason the Deli-choices Rolls are so high in sugar is primarily the tomato sauce, so if you are a fan and don't want to give them up, scrape the sauce off first (I'd pay to see you do that). Coffee- and tea-based drinks come in at zero sugar (after adjusting for lactose) but this doesn't give you carte blanche at McCafe; do not order anything that involves a flavouring because a serious whack of sugar comes in the flavouring syrup.

Lunch and dinner

Some of us like a hot lunch and others prefer a hot dinner, so I've lumped these two together. You may rearrange them according to habit.

Sandwiches

Any kind of sandwich that involves a low-fructose bread (see page 118), butter (or none – up to you) and a spread that isn't sweet (such as Vegemite, peanut butter without added salt or cream cheese) is fine. For those with the time and inclination towards salad sangers, any of the salad vegies are fine. (The worst, from a fructose perspective, is tomato, and that barely rates.) And you may add any meat you wish.

Roast meat or ham sandwiches are great for the carnivores as long as you don't add relishes, most of which are high in sugar (see page 123). The good news is that mustards are either completely sugar-free or, in the case of wholegrain varieties, very low in sugar. Most gravy is also sugar-free (being largely flour, water and fat). And mayonnaise is fine, too, as long as it is whole-egg and full-fat (see page 124). Unfortunately, most sandwich shops and salad bars use 'traditional' low-fat mayonnaise (often over 20 per cent sugar). If you find one that uses full-fat whole-egg mayo, stick to it like glue. (Or, ask your local hangout to switch – you never know your luck in the big city.) Any kind of egg sandwich is good.

Salads

Salads are great as long as you are careful with the dressing. Most shop-bought dressings are unreasonably high in sugar (see page 125). It is worth looking at the labels, though, because sugar content varies considerably, even between the same types of dressing. Always avoid the low-fat or fat-free versions; they usually contain an extra 3–5 g of sugar per 100 g. A great and easy alternative is to simply make your own. Mix a little olive oil with wholegrain mustard or lime/lemon juice, throw in some herbs for taste and *voila*! Instant, sugar-free (or very close to) salad dressing.

Asian food

Asian food can be a bit of a tricky proposition for the recovering sugarholic. Brown sugar is often a primary ingredient in Thai sauces and an important component in others. And since sauces tend to be the essence of much Asian food, this can be a problem. If you are cooking at home, be selective about which brand of sauce you use because the sugar content varies significantly between brands. But if you are eating out, these two guidelines will help:

Rules for eating out Asian-style

1. When possible, stick to Chinese or Indian cuisine rather than going for Thai or Malaysian.
2. Stay away from anything that mentions honey or sweet chilli.

Here's a sample of some of the more popular sauces and pastes used as recipe foundations for Asian foods.

Common Asian sauces & pastes	% sugar
Hoi sin sauce	25–50
Sweet chilli sauce	43–49
Sweet-and-sour sauce; pad Thai paste	30
Oyster sauce	25
Satay sauce	22
Thai red curry paste	10–20
Nasi goreng sauce	14
Sambal sauce	12
Blackbean sauce	10
Laksa sauce	5–10
Malaysian, Thai green & tikka masala curry pastes	8
Korma curry paste	7
Rendang sauce	6
Madras, vindaloo and rogan josh curry pastes	5
Tandoori curry paste	1
Soy sauce	1
Thai massaman curry paste	1

The key to Asian food is the curry pastes, and the various herbs and spices. There is a huge (and constantly changing) range of brands for most of these pastes but it won't take you long to locate a version with half the sugar content of all the others at your local supermarket. You don't have to go cold turkey on Asian food; you just have to know that it is dangerous territory and that you are risking significant exposure to sugar if you eat out.

I'm a fan of Asian foods. I'm new to sugar-free (day 5 now), but I've been spending a lot of time reading the labels of everything in my pantry and at the supermarket.

I was shocked to find, last night, that my brand of hoi sin sauce had sugar listed as the very first ingredient! Similarly, I have found that nearly every other Asian sauce I once cooked with is laced with sugar. I have decided to kick the sugar habit completely if I can, so out the door goes fish sauce, kecap manis, hoi sin, sweet chilli (of course), satay paste, laksa paste, all other curry pastes and even the brand of soy sauce I buy. I'm switching to tamari and making my sauces from scratch.

I am pretty certain it would be very hard indeed to buy take-away Asian foods without sugar. I'll have a chat to the folk at my local noodle joint next time I'm there.

Raegose

Takeaway

The danger in takeaway food lies largely in the condiments, the desserts and the drinks. Here are a few simple rules for takeaway.

Rules for takeaway

1. Stay away from the drinks fridge – there's nothing to see here (unless you feel like paying a lot for water).
2. Don't even think about the ice-cream fridge.
3. Don't buy sauces to go with the meal and if the sauce usually comes on board (such as with a hamburger), ask for your meal to be made without sauce.

Observe these rules and your – now functional – appetite control system will limit how much you can eat of everything else. You will be surprised to discover that, as you get into withdrawal, you'll consume less and less every time you visit the takeaway shop.

McDonald's and similar fast-food

Once again, just because they publish such gloriously detailed lists of the sugar content of their foods, I'll use McDonald's as an example of the things to watch out for in the fast-food 'restaurant'.

It's a rare person who goes to Macca's without visions of a burger. So, that's a logical place to start. Here is a list of all the McDonald's burger offerings, ranked by sugar content per serve (one serve = one burger). Because the burgers are different sizes, the percentage of sugar is different to the teaspoon ranking. Even when taking into account all that sauce, there isn't a single burger which will slug you with more than two teaspoons of sugar. And you will eat less than a teaspoon of sugar by having any of the top seven choices (which are all chicken- or fish-based). If you really want to lower the sugar content of the rest, then order your burger without sauce or be ready with a scraping knife when you (of course) remove the pickle.

McDonald's burger	% sugar	Sugar (tsp)
Filet-o-Fish	1.9	0.50
McChicken	1.7	0.75
Classic Seared Chicken	2.0	1.00
Crispy Chicken Deluxe	1.7	1.00
Crispy Chicken Bacon Deluxe	1.8	1.00
Grand Angus	1.6	1.00
Seared Chicken Deluxe	1.9	1.00
Hamburger	4.7	1.00
Cheeseburger	4.3	1.00
Seared Chicken Bacon Deluxe	2.0	1.25
Double Cheeseburger	3.1	1.25
Big Mac	2.8	1.25
Quarter Pounder	3.2	1.50
Double Quarter Pounder	2.2	1.50
Mighty Angus	3.5	2.25

The wraps aren't too sugary, either, as long as you avoid anything with 'sweet chilli' in its name.

McDonald's wrap	% sugar	Sugar (tsp)
Seared Chicken Snack	1.6	0.25
Crispy Chicken Snack	2.7	0.75
Deli-choices Seared Chicken Caesar	2.1	1.00
Tick Approved Chicken Tandoori Deli-choices Crispy Chicken Caesar	2.5 3.3	1.50
Tick Approved Chicken Sweet Chilli	6.7	3.50
Deli-Choices Crispy Chicken Sweet Chilli	7.9	4.25

You can safely add fries and nuggets to your order. There isn't any sugar in French fries and you would need to eat 60 McNuggets to consume one teaspoon of sugar. However, if you can't eat a McNugget without a dipping sauce then you are in sugar trouble (see McDonald's condiments list on page 146).

Getting a low-sugar drink at Macca's is a little tricky, although now that they sell water, that is always an option. Most of the rest of the drink menu leaves a lot to be desired if you don't like artificial sweeteners or hot drinks. The milk-based drinks in this list have been adjusted to allow for lactose (i.e. I have reduced the sugar content on the label by 4.7 per cent). Here are the drinks ranked from lowest sugar per serve to highest.

McDonald's drink	% sugar (adjusted for lactose)	Sugar (tsp), adjusted for lactose
Diet Coke	0.0	0.0
Spring Water	0.0	0.0
All coffee- and tea-based drinks	0.0	0.0
Regular Iced Coffee	1.4	1.75
CalciYum Chocolate Milk	3.5	2.00
Large Iced Coffee	1.4	2.25
Small Fruit Fizz	5.5	4.00
Small Sprite Strawberry Nudie	7.6 9.4	5.50
Medium Fruit Fizz Small Goulburn Valley Orange Juice	5.7 8.2	5.75
Small Chocolate Shake Small Coke	8.5 9.3	6.25
Small Vanilla Shake Small Strawberry Shake	8.8 8.9	6.50

Extra Juicy Apple Juice	11.0	6.50
Small Fanta	10.1	7.25
Medium Sprite Mango Nudie	8.1 13.5	8.00
Medium Goulburn Valley Orange Juice Medium Coke	8.2 8.8	8.50
Large Fruit Fizz	6.0	8.75
Regular Frozen Fanta Raspberry	13.5	9.75
Regular Frozen Coke	13.5	10.25
Medium Fanta	10.7	10.25
Large Chocolate Shake	8.5	11.50
Large Vanilla Shake	8.8	11.75
Large Strawberry Shake	8.9	12.00
Large Sprite	8.6	12.00
Large Coke Large Frozen Fanta Raspberry	9.3 13.5	13.00
Large Frozen Coke	13.5	13.25
Large Fanta	11.4	16.00

You won't be having dessert at McDonald's. But just in case you're curious, here they are (once again adjusted for lactose). If you really can't get through a meal without dessert, then I recommend you stick to the Apple Pie.

McDonald's dessert	% sugar (adjusted for lactose)	Sugar (tsp), adjusted for lactose
Apple Pie	8.6	1.75
Ice-cream Party Cake (slice)	16.3	
Soft-Serve Cone	14.9	3.25
McDonaldland Cookies	27.6	4.00
Sundae (no topping)	15.9	5.00
Regular Strawberry Sundae	21.3	8.75
Regular Hot Caramel Sundae	20.8	8.75
McFlurry with Oreo Cookies	16.8	8.75
Regular Hot Fudge Sundae	22.5	9.25
McFlurry with M&M Minis	20.5	11.25
Large Strawberry Sundae	22.8	13.00
Large Hot Caramel Sundae	23.1	13.75
Double Choc Party Cake (slice)	35.3	14.00
Large Hot Fudge Sundae	26.1	15.25

A while ago, McDonald's introduced 'healthier' options ('Tick-Approved', i.e. given the approval of the Heart Foundation) to lure the more health-conscious of us through the door. But these options are said to be 'healthier' because they are low-fat, and in many cases, sugar makes an unwelcome and unhealthy appearance via dressings (see table opposite).

McDonald's menu item	% sugar	Sugar (tsp)
Caesar Salad Dressing	3.1	0.25
Garden Salad (no dressing)	1.3	
Crispy Chicken Caesar with Bagel Chips (no dressing)	0.9	0.50
Seared Chicken Caesar with Bagel Chips (no dressing)	1.0	
Italian Salad Dressing	9.8	0.75
Crispy Classic Chicken with Bagel Chips (no dressing)	0.9	
Crispy Classic Chicken with Bagel Chips (no dressing)	1.0	
Balsamic Salad Dressing	9.4	1.00
Apple Slices	11.5	1.75
Tick Approved Filet-o-Fish, Garden Salad and Italian Dressing	2.6	
Tick Approved McChicken, Garden Salad and Italian Dressing	2.4	
Tick Approved Hamburger, Garden Salad and Italian Dressing	3.8	2.25
Tick Approved Chicken Tandoori Wrap, Garden Salad and Italian Dressing	2.8	2.50
Tick Approved 6 pc McNuggets, Garden Salad and Italian Dressing	4.0	
Tick Approved Seared Chicken Sweet Chilli Wrap, Garden Salad and Italian Dressing	4.6	4.00

While many of the meals above are very low in sugar, a sugar avoider can come undone in the condiment department. A low-sugar lifestyle means learning to eat a Macca's meal without smothering it in any of the following. If you can stop at one serve (one sachet) you might not do too much harm, but remember that each sachet contains the number of teaspoons of sugar you see in the table on page 146.

McDonald's condiment	% sugar	Sugar (tsp)
Creamy Ranch Dipping Sauce	4.5	0.25
Ketchup	20.5	0.50
Mustard	20.3	1.25
Honey Mustard Dipping Sauce BBQ Sauce	34.1 31.2	2.00
Sweet & Sour Sauce	35.8	2.50

Pizza

Depending how much of it you eat, pizza is a fairly low-sugar option. The sauce is the primary source ('scuse pun) of the sugar, so the generosity of the sauce purveyor is what makes all the difference. Because 'BBQ meat lover's' pizzas use barbecue sauce, they tend to be the highest-sugar pizzas. Hawaiian pizzas include pineapple and, once again depending on generosity, this can push their sugar rating up. Pepperoni pizzas are generally the lowest-sugar option because they are just meat and a straight tomato sauce. These numbers apply equally across most takeaway outlets, although Pizza Hut is consistently at the high end of the (sugar) scale.

Pizza	% sugar
Garlic bread Pepperoni	0–3 1–4
Vegetarian supreme	2–5
BBQ meat lover's	2–6
Hawaiian	3–6

A standard (takeaway) piece of pizza weighs about 80 g, so one piece of BBQ meatlover's or Hawaiian could give you up to one teaspoon of sugar. But a reasonable rule of thumb is that there is half a teaspoon of sugar (1 g of fructose) in every slice of pizza you buy. It's best to limit yourself to two standard slices (eventually, you won't be able to eat that much anyway). Garlic breads vary between nothing and around 3 per cent sugar, based on the bread used, which is usually a white roll of some description.

Note that these ranges are for hot takeaway pizzas, not frozen pizzas from the supermarket. Most frozen pizzas contain around 10 per cent sugar, which is a significant increase. Most of this is added sugar in the pizza base and a higher-than-usual sugar content for the sauce. One 80 g slice of the average supermarket frozen pizza will feed you about two teaspoons of sugar. If you're shopping for dinner in the freezer section and have an aversion to vegetables, then meat pies and sausage rolls are a far superior option to pizza. Most brands have barely any sugar (but it's worth a quick look at the label); they rely on you adding the sugar when you get home via your trusty bottle of tomato sauce. But if you use the sauce recipe in chapter 5, you'll have yourself a nice little sugar-free dinner. I wouldn't make it an every-night affair or the lack of fibre will, er, catch up with you. But as an occasional dinner option, there's nothing wrong with the traditional Aussie meat pie.

Rather than buying frozen pizzas, make your own – it's relatively easy to make a good pizza using unsweetened scone dough as the base (see chapter 5) and the lowest-sugar tomato paste you can find. (Be careful with the pastes – they vary enormously in sugar content. For example, Ardmona Rich and Thick is only 8.5 per cent sugar whereas Coles Italian is 20.3 per cent.) A thin smear of paste with any topping you like from your sugar-free cupboards and fridge will make a great, almost totally fructose-free meal.

The other item you will increasingly find in takeaway pizza shops is pasta dishes. The white-sauced ones (e.g. alfredo) will feed you about one teaspoon of sugar per serve (300 g) and the red-sauced ones (e.g. napoli) will double that. While these dishes are not ideal, they are not cause for real concern. I wouldn't panic about the sugar in anything in a pizza shop except the desserts and the drinks – as long as you're not eating there every night.

Restaurants

All of this advice about pizza takeaways applies in general to Italian restaurants. Most of the food you will encounter there is largely low-sugar and won't bother you unless you eat out regularly. Just watch out for the balsamic vinegar they serve to dip your bread in.

With most other kinds of restaurants, the obvious danger is the dessert menu – but it's easy to avoid. Many restaurants offer a cheese platter with coffee. Make a habit of ordering that instead of dessert and you'll be fine. That's what I did to start with. But as my appetite control adjusted, I found myself feeling stuffed by the end of the main and just went for coffee. This was a very visible symptom of the changes that were occurring in the new sugar-free me. I was going to the same restaurants and ordering the same meals (I'm boring like that. What can I say? I like steak), but was feeling like an overstuffed sofa before I'd even finished the meal. Previously, I'd been able to eat the whole thing, knock off dessert and still feel like having something else. The waiters seemed to be peering down their noses at me when I started skipping dessert – I'm sure they suspected my reasons were financial rather than dietary, especially when I gave up the entree as well!

Get in the habit of ordering mineral water instead of a flavoured drink/juice, or stick to table water or a low-sugar alcohol (such as red wine). The only other danger area on most menus is the mayo. Avoid things smothered in mayonnaise (like BLTs) unless you know it is whole-egg full-fat. If you don't know the restaurant and you get a pile of mayo on everything, it's usually easy to scrape it off. (And at least you'll remember to order it without mayo next time.) Don't worry too much about most other sauces. Most restaurants pride themselves on creating tomato sauce from fresh tomatoes, and most kinds of *jus* are just too watery to worry about (and generally low in sugar, anyway).

Rules for eating out

1. Order a cheese platter instead of dessert.
2. Stick to mineral water or low-sugar alcohol.
3. Stay away from balsamic vinegar.
4. Avoid mayonnaise-based sauces.

Cooking at home

Since you've re-stocked your larder and fridge according to the guides in **Step 5**, you can pretty much cook whatever you want for lunch or dinner. This is why it's important to make sure that you only have sugar-free food in the house. Your kitchen becomes a haven, where you know that every available ingredient is sugar-free. You can combine anything with anything, knowing that whatever you cook for yourself and those you love will not be poisoning you or them. Any kind of meat with any kind of vegetable makes for a good meal. You can have pasta, potatoes or rice with anything and know that if you are careful about the sauces, anything goes. (Remember that if you are going Asian, veer towards Indian rather than Thai. And if you're going with generic curry, use curry powder rather than a prepared paste.) If you've stocked up on low-sugar bread, then any kind of sandwich is also on the menu.

Dessert

Since you're not allowed to eat dessert at restaurants, you're not allowed to buy ice-cream at the supermarket and you not allowed to get ice-creams at the takeaway shop, you might be thinking you've eaten your last dessert. Happily, that is not the case (as long as you can cook or you know someone who will cook for you). Many of the recipes in chapter 5 are devoted to solving the problem of dessert. For almost everything you eat other than dessert, you will be able to find a commercial product that has significantly less or no sugar, if you look hard enough. But when it comes to dessert, you are fresh out of luck. The good news is, however, that by using the recipes in chapter 5, you will be able to recreate almost all your favourites using dextrose instead of sugar. The recipes are based on full-sugar recipes that Lizzie has tweaked and modified (sometimes sig-nificantly) to make them taste exactly the same as the full-sugar original. Well, that's not exactly true. If you eat these recipes before you start withdrawal (which you shouldn't – see the warning on page 129), they will taste bland; but after you've broken the addic-tion, they will taste as you remember the full-sugar versions tasting. And some of them (like the ice-creams) would fool even the most hardened sugar addict. If a dessert you love is not there, then pay close attention to the proportions of dextrose in something similar and you will be able to modify your favourite recipe.

The interesting thing about dessert and sweets in general is that after you have completed withdrawal, they really do lose much of their appeal. Once you are no longer addicted to sugar, you'll be able to take or leave dextrose-based desserts. This is not to say they don't taste great (they do), but your attitude to that kind of food changes. Sure, you'll eat it and you'll enjoy every last mouthful, but unlike sugar-based foods, they won't leave you wanting more. It's hard to believe, I know, but it does happen to everybody who completes withdrawal. Most people tell me that they like having a few dextrose recipes around for birthday parties and for when sugar-addicted guests drop over, but that's about it.

A typical day

You can eat anything you like if you follow the rules I've set out previously (see page 168 for a summary). Once you give up sugar and your appetite control starts to function again, you will suddenly find yourself feeling unexpectedly and uncomfortably full. It will be a new experience for you. Prior to withdrawal, I do not recall ever in my life feeling full the way I feel full now. And if you do consciously overeat, you will find yourself feeling ill for hours afterwards.

Although you can eat what you like from your sugar-free fridge and pantry, sometimes it helps to have some idea of how to structure your fructose-free day. So, here's a sample day in the life of a recovering sugarholic (no prizes for guessing who).

Meal	Approximate fructose content (g)
Breakfast	
2 pieces of Bürgen rye toast (with butter and Vegemite) and a glass of full-cream milk	0.7 (from the bread and Vegemite)
Morning tea	
A handful of cashews (35) and a glass of water	1.3
Lunch	
Two rounds of ham, cheese and lettuce (on sourdough with butter) and a glass of water	0.1 (from the lettuce)
Afternoon tea	
1 sliced pear	4.5
Dinner	
Roast beef with roast vegetables (potato, broccoli and carrot) and a glass of dry white wine	1.5 (mostly from the carrot)
Total for the day	8.1

There are three important things to notice about this sample day:

1. The total fructose content for the day is about the same as one apple.
2. None of the fructose comes without a whacking great serve of fibre. The bread is high-fibre, the nuts are high-fibre, and even the biggest donor (the pear) is one of the highest-fibre fruits.
3. You could halve the fructose content by simply deleting the pear. The world wouldn't end, but you might begin to have some problems in the smallest room in the house.

This is no longer a typical day for me. When I started going sugar-free, I ate morning and afternoon tea because it didn't affect my appetite and I was in the habit of doing it. Now it is very rare. Since finishing withdrawal, I no longer desire the snack. This was neither a conscious nor a sudden change. Because I became less and less focused on food after withdrawal, I would sometimes forget to have a snack. After a while (this might have taken a year or so), the forgetting became more common than the remembering and before I knew it, snacks were very much the exception. When I did have a snack, I found that it so significantly impacted my appetite that I would end up being unable to eat all of the next meal. But at the start of withdrawal, this sample is a good framework for what to put into a daily meal plan, even if your (increasingly functional) appetite control system eventually forces you to delete some items.

If you substituted a pie for lunch and a restaurant meal for dinner, you wouldn't change the outcome much, as long as you avoided sugary drinks and dessert. The quantities you are able to eat of any of these things will be affected as your appetite control returns. For example, if you decide to have two handfuls of cashews for morning tea, you won't be eating two rounds of sangars for lunch. Why? Because I come round and stop you? No. Because you exercise willpower? No. Because your appetite control system will let you know (in no uncertain terms) that you've had enough after the first round.

The other big change you'll notice once you complete withdrawal is that food becomes less of a central concern in your life. You'll eat to live rather than living to eat. This doesn't mean you won't enjoy it; on the contrary, I found myself developing a sense of taste I didn't know I had when sugar masked everything. You'll enjoy it more, but it will be about the flavours rather than the quantity or the sweetness. You'll eat when you're hungry and really won't think about it much at any other time. This was certainly a new experience for me and hundreds of people have confirmed it since the release of *Sweet Poison*.

What's for lunch, Mum and Dad?

If you don't have kids, feel free to skip this section. Although if you have to pack yourself a lunch for work, you might learn a thing or two.

Sugary-food manufacturers know that time-poor parents just want to know that they can feed their kids a nutritious meal or snack. They also know that the sweeter they make the meal or snack, the more likely the child is to want to eat it. The end result is foods with nutrition messages on the outside (packaging) and sugar on the inside. Your kids should be eating the same things you are (and not eating the same things you aren't), but don't expect them to appreciate you removing the sugar from their lives. This does not mean you shouldn't tell them about the evils of sugar; information has been proven to make a big difference when it comes to children and sugar.

Education, prohibition, or both?

A very interesting study was conducted in the UK in 2001 to see what difference a little sugar knowledge made to children's health. In the study, 644 schoolchildren from 32 schools were divided into two groups. One group (the intervention group) was told they would be healthier if they stopped drinking sugar (in the form of soft drinks). The control group (who were at different schools) were not told; they were simply given the normal 'don't eat fat and exercise more' message. In the intervention group, the sugar message was delivered on only four occasions (one lesson per term), during one of the regular weekly health and physical education lessons. That lesson was devoted to the 'drink less sugar' message while every other weekly health lesson was as per normal.

The control group, who weren't told about sugar, got fatter. By the end of the school year, there were 7.5 per cent more overweight and obese kids in that group than there were at the start. In the intervention group, there were slightly fewer (0.2 per cent) overweight and obese kids than at the start. No one was forcing the children to stop drinking sugar and they didn't entirely stop; they just slightly reduced the amount they drank on average. Four hours invested over the course of a year had prevented a whole bunch of kids being a lot fatter than they otherwise would have been. Armed guards and Rottweilers were not needed. The kids were simply given information about the dangers of sugar.

Another recent study out of Yale University tried a tactic most parents would be reluctant to attempt. Instead of educating children, they just removed sugar-filled food as an option. The researchers looked at a group of 89 kids (aged 5–12) and what they ate when they were away at summer camp. Half the group were offered only low-sugar cereals (the American equivalent of Weet-Bix etc.) and the other half were offered only high-sugar cereals. Both groups had access to as much table sugar, strawberries, bananas and fruit juice as they wanted.

The Yale team wanted to know firstly whether the children offered low-sugar cereals would protest and refuse breakfast. Perhaps surprisingly, 100 per cent of the low-sugar group just ate what was on offer. (Of the high-sugar group, 1 per cent refused – obviously some aberrant child snuck in!) The interesting thing is that the low-sugar group ate a lot less than the high-sugar group – in fact, they ate half as much. On average, the low-sugar group ate the recommended serving of the cereal (one cup). But the high-sugar group ate on average two cups. The low-sugar group compensated for less cereal by adding table sugar to their cereal and drinking more juice, but even when that was included in the calculations, they ate significantly less sugar than the kids munching on the high-sugar cereal. The researchers didn't do it, but an interesting extension to this study would be to remove the table sugar and juice, making sure there was plenty of cold milk to drink. I rather suspect the result would be even more impressive. My guess would be that the kids would once again eat what was on offer, perhaps eating less cereal and drinking more milk, but their sugar consumption would be insignificant.

The researchers also asked the children to rate their breakfasts out of five (with 1 being the best). The high-sugar kids rated theirs 1.5, on average. You might have expected a less satisfied result from the low-sugar kids but their average was 1.6. The interesting thing about this study is that it did what many parents find very difficult: it simply removed the option. There was no attempt at moderation or education. The kids weren't unhappy. And they didn't starve. They just moved on with the new reality. Combining what these two studies tell us provokes some interesting thought. Prohibition works and education works. Combine prohibition with education and we might just have the recipe for healthy, sugar-free kids.

But my kids aren't fat

As a proportion of the population, fewer children are overweight than adults. Almost two-thirds of adults are either overweight or obese, compared with just one-quarter of children. But having any significant number of fat kids is a relatively new thing. In 1985, just one in ten Aussie kids was overweight or obese. In a quarter of a century, we've more than doubled that figure to one in four. Even so, if you are the parent of one of the other three in four, you might be feeling a little smug. But beware: kids don't need to be fat to be suffering the damage done by sugar.

Growing children use vastly more energy than adults (relative to their size). Their brain size (for the first 12 or so years) relative to their body size means that they require much more pure energy than adults do. A toddler uses 45 per cent of his energy just keeping his brain running. Adults only use 25 per cent (and some of us, I dare say, probably considerably less than that). On top of that, children need to build a body. A two-year-old needs to consume 65 per cent of the calories of an adult woman. By the time he hits four, he requires 90 per cent, and by seven, 100 per cent. They'll get those calories from anywhere – sugar, fat, whatever you feed them.

To eat more than they need and start to put some away for later is actually quite a feat for children. Most wouldn't be able to accomplish it without the appetite-control-dimming effect of fructose. But just because three-quarters of them (so far) are not getting fat doesn't mean that sugar is not doing damage. Uric acid is still being produced, which ramps up their blood pressure and damages the kidneys. Arteries are still being filled with fatty acids that push them towards insulin-resistance, PCOS and, ultimately, diabetes. Collagen and elastin are still being messed up, pushing them towards flabbiness and low skin tone. For young girls, the protective effect of oestrogen is yet to kick in. And, perhaps worst of all, children's appetite control is being blunted to the point where they will habitually overconsume. So when they stop growing, stand back for the fat explosion.

There is one fairly reliable way to tell whether your kids are consuming too much sugar. Researchers have known since the sixties that tooth decay is caused by a little chap called *Streptococcus mutans* (SM). It is one of the 200–300 species of bacteria that inhabit our mouths. SM is a little unusual, though. It's rather like a koala in that it only really likes one thing to eat. No, not gum leaves. SM wants sugar. To be more precise, SM likes the two components of sugar, glucose and fructose, in exactly the proportions they are found in sugar (50:50). In hundreds of well-controlled studies, scientists have been able to determine that feeding sugar to SM causes

It's now many years ago, but I always restricted sugar with my children. As they grew up and we moved into city life, it was harder, but the early beginning helped. All have good teeth and none are overweight. And I did not know fructose was the evil part in those days. We had eggs for breakfast etc.

It is much harder today, there is no doubt. Now, with grandchildren, I explain to them about bad foods and there is no doubt they are influenced by example. When a friend gave them marshmallows, I offered them a choice – the money or the lollies – and they chose the money! Lollies went into bin. I never give lollies or chocolates for presents. You can hard-boil eggs and paint the outside for Easter. Make it fun.

I sometimes draw a diagram to explain the sugar molecule. I'd also advise using the 'no lollies today' method rather than saying 'never'. Better that they voluntarily avoid sugar because of education. Sash had too much fruit juice for a while and he knows what happened to his early teeth.

Wise23girl

it to produce plaque (the gummy coating on teeth) and lactic acid. If you feed pure glucose or fructose to SM, it can only produce the acid; it can't make plaque without sugar and without plaque there is no decay. (Lactic acid damages the enamel on your teeth, but it is the plaque that holds the acid against the tooth's surface. Without the plaque, the acid is washed away quickly by your saliva.) If you want to rot teeth, the most effective way is to provide SM with a constant wash of sugar solution (like soft drink, fruit juice or flavoured yoghurt). Eating sugar in solid food is also damaging but it is nowhere near as effective at helping SM do its job because a lot of it ends up in your tummy before SM can get to it.

SM has really enjoyed our change in diet since World War II. The amount of sugar-laden soft drinks, juice and flavoured milk we drink has risen from virtually nothing to almost 1 litre per person per day. Consumption of soft drink alone has more than doubled in the last 30 years. So, even if your child is managing (so far) not to get fat on a high-sugar diet, there's a good chance that (unless they are a teeth-cleaning machine) they will be part of the swelling crowd of children requiring significant dental work before they are 12 years old.

Getting kids off sugar is about discipline. Not theirs, yours. The home environment is where you have the most control. If you've gone through the steps above, you will have a largely sugar-free house. You will know that the kids can eat anything in your cupboard or fridge and not get any sugar. But controlling the world outside your house may prove to be a little problematic. For that, you need rules. The rules need to be logical and they need to be clearly (and repeatedly) explained. These rules will not prevent your little darlings from sucking down some sugar when they get the chance, but they might stop them going back for seconds and overall help to moderate them towards a sugar-free palate. Of course, you have to lead by example. You can't be seen to prohibit sweets at Macca's and then chow down on an ice-cream cone yourself. Nor can you prohibit sweets on the way home from school and then cave in at the first checkout queue (and some persistent nagging, no doubt).

Useful rules for helping children avoid sugar

All of these must be accompanied by a clear explanation as to why you are prohibiting sugar, set out in terms that your children will understand and which clearly affect them.

1. **Ensure the house is sugar-free**. This must be absolute. If you have any cracks in the sugar-free wall at home, kids (like sheep looking for a break in the fence) will exploit that weakness and soon you will be back where you started. If you are firm (and unwavering) about this, kids will accept the new reality a lot quicker than you think.

2. **Make sure the lunchbox is sugar-free**. Most primary-school kids are supervised at lunchtime and are not allowed to throw food out. If they're hungry, they'll eat what you give them. If they don't eat it, they weren't hungry and they are coming home to a sugar-free house (and afternoon tea) anyway.

3. **Don't ban the tuckshop**. Banning anything only seems to make it more attractive! Instead, know the tuckshop menu and help your children choose carefully. They will occasionally choose the wrong thing but that's not the end of the world. Most kids will try hard to obey your rules and when they don't, they'll feel guilty about it and probably won't make a habit of it.

4. **Don't be afraid of the new**. When Pumpkin comes home with a tale of woe that Muffy had [insert name of new treat] in her lunchbox, don't automatically say no. Check it out. It might be sugar-free or very low in sugar. You'd be surprised. And if it isn't sugar-free, explain that that's the reason you're saying no; you'll be surprised how accepting children can be.

5. **Find another way to reward children**. Food rewards are easy and mindless, but should be restricted to circus animals. Your kids deserve better. If they have balanced a ball on their nose

for an hour, reward them with a trip to the movies rather than an ice-cream. Food is fuel, not a reward.

6. **Prepare them for parties**. If you know they are going into an environment where sugar consumption will be mandatory, talk to them about why it's not a good idea to have too much. Ask them to have just one fizzy drink or juice then switch to water or diet soft drinks if they're available. Ask them to veer towards the chippie bowl and away from the sweets. Maybe they'll have more than one drink, but if they do, they'll have your words ringing in their ears. Don't prohibit them from bringing home a party bag, but do ration the consumption of the bag's contents.

7. **Don't make a teenager stick out**. Teenage kids would rather throw themselves in front of a bus than not do what everyone else is doing. Give them some secret rules that they can follow without looking like a weirdo. Tell them that when their friends are guzzling soft drink, they should choose cool, youth-oriented diet versions like Coke Zero and Pepsi Max. (If anyone asks, they can say they prefer the taste.) When they're hanging at Macca's, get the diet drink and the apple pie for dessert (if they must). When they're heading for a sleepover (aka sugarthon), pack a bottle of diet soft drink and a bag of crisps as gifts for the host; that way, even if there aren't any other low-sugar options, your child will at least have a choice. (It also teaches them that it's nice to contribute something.)

You can't expect children to never taste sugar. They will go to parties and they will have treats. And, being children, they will chow down with the rest of their mates. If you've had them on a no-sugar (or low-sugar) diet, they won't be used to the fructose and may well find much of the food too sweet, but they'll still probably eat it. Don't panic.

Rule 5: Party food is for parties

This rule seems to work well with kids. Sure, they love party food, but it's an extra-special treat for them because they don't get it every other day of the week.

I'm no professional child wrangler, but it seems to me that you've got to give kids a little room to adjust. Don't expect them to elect you parent of the month, but remember that eventually they do adjust to the reality that sugar is no longer part of your (or their) lives. And the older they get, the more they appreciate why.

All of that being said, there are some things you can do to dramatically reduce the sugar in children's lives without making them feel like martyrs.

Breakfast for kids

For breakfast, the kids need to be weaned off high-sugar cereals and spreads, and moved to the low-sugar options set out above. My eldest daughter (10) loved her Sultana Bran (22.7% sugar). Now she eats Weet-Bix instead. Getting her there wasn't instant; it was a combination of removing alternatives and the long-term removal of sugar from the rest of her life. A child of her age is capable of understanding why she shouldn't have five teaspoons of sugar for breakfast. As we removed sugar from the rest of our lives and her tastebuds began adjusting to a less sweet level, she could taste how sweet Sultana Bran really was. We told her that when she'd finished the box, she'd need to have something else for breakfast, and we stopped buying it. We tried buying All-bran and adding (a limited quantity of) sultanas ourselves, but there was still a huge amount of sugar in the All-Bran (13.6%), so we decided to limit her options to the 10 lowest-sugar breakfast cereals available (see page 71). She chose Weet-Bix and it was a smooth transition. Weet-Bix still has some sugar (2.5%) but it is a massive reduction and she is getting plenty of fibre along with it. She'll still dig into the Sultana Bran at a Sizzler breakfast, but that's only a couple of times a year. The rest of the time, she happily eats an extremely low-sugar breakfast.

Children will not starve to prove a point. If the only thing on offer is Weet-Bix or wholegrain toast, they'll generally choose one or the other. And if it's clear that the situation will not be changing, they very quickly find the thing they like the most and stick with it. Around our breakfast table we have one child who eats cheese on toast (usually cheddar but sometimes cream cheese, for a change); two who eat avocado on toast; one who has Weet-Bix and buttered toast; and two who have Vegemite toast. (These two used to have a bowl of Woolworths Home Brand Corn Flakes, too, but Woolies have recently increased the sugar content on this product to 9 per cent, probably in a bid to compete with their sweeter rivals.) The toast is multigrain bread and is buttered with butter, not margarine. And everyone has a glass of full-cream milk.

In winter, a few of our children switch to porridge (unflavoured rolled oats) made with milk and sometimes half a banana. None of it is terribly exciting, but it's all filling and they don't miss the old days too much. They used to eat Milo Cereal, Nutrigrain and even occasionally Coco Pops. But these items are simply no longer available in our pantry and the kids enjoy the new range of possibilities without (much) grumbling. Avocado is just about the best thing you can spread on a piece of toast. It is high in fibre and has almost no sugar. If I had my way, they'd all be eating that, but then I'd have to start committing armed robberies just to keep up with the grocery bills. Vegemite is a good alternative that kids tend to like (as long as they have been raised on it).

School lunches

School lunches have to fulfil two primary requirements for parents: they have to be quick to put together and they should end up in the child and not in the bin. Food manufacturers know that little individual packages take care of the first bit and a tonne of sugar takes care of the second bit.

Unfortunately, there is almost no snack or muesli bar (one of the most popular items for school lunches) that you can throw in a lunchbox without feeding your child a huge amount of sugar (see pages 73–5). Even things such as dipping packs of cheese and crackers, which on the surface appear unlikely to contain sugar, can sometimes contain surprisingly large amounts. There are, however, a few products, such as Mainland's Cheddar Cheese and Rice Crackers, which contain no sugar or only a very small amount. Anything containing dried fruit or sweets is off your list, but anything containing just crackers (preferably unflavoured) and cheese is likely to be okay. Our kids don't mind having plain old crackers. Twenty Arnott's BBQ Shapes (46 g) contain less than a gram of sugar. Plain crackers (like Sao or unflavoured rice crackers) are even better.

If you prefer muesli bars then stick to the fruit-free varieties such as Carman's Original Fruit-free. They are not completely without sugar because they need something to hold the thing together, but their sugar content is very low. Unflavoured popcorn is a great sugar-free morning tea that stays edible in a schoolbag. Either buy the corn kernels yourself, pop them in a saucepan (with a bit of olive oil) and put them in snap-seal baggies, or just buy unflavoured popped corn.

Fresh fruit is a good choice, especially if you can veer towards the bottom right of Figure 2.5 (see page 108) with fruits such as pears, kiwi fruit and berries (perhaps leave the lemons out). Bear in mind that children should not have any more than one serve of fruit per day, so this will be it. Berries are often a good choice for kids. They like the no-fuss, pop-it-in-your-mouth feature. However, berries can often be hideously expensive. One way around this is to buy the packs of frozen berries available from the supermarket freezer; they are often less than half the price and are just about at room temperature by the time morning tea rolls around.

School lunch do's and don'ts		
	Don't use	Do use
Morning tea	Prepackaged muesli bars or snack bars	Fruit-free muesli bars, unflavoured popcorn, cheese and cracker dipping packs or plain crackers
Lunch	Packaged cakes or yoghurts	Homemade sandwiches or bread rolls
	Packaged fruit snacks (such as Uncle Tobys Fruit Fix)	Fresh fruit or frozen berries
Drinks	Juices or soft drinks	Water
Other options	Sweets	Nuts or 'fish and chips' (see page 166) Pikelets (use the Pancakes recipe on page 243)

For lunch, sandwiches or rolls are the way to go. Unfortunately, you are unlikely to have time to mess around with them before school. But if you do just a little prep on the weekends, things become a lot easier. For example, make up a bunch of avocado (or chicken or ham or Vegemite or cheese) bread rolls on Sunday afternoon and throw them all in the freezer straight away. Then dole them out through the week. They thaw beautifully by lunchtime in a schoolbag and have the added advantage of keeping the drink cool. One lunchtime treat that has become popular with our kids is 'fish and chips': a small tin of canned tuna (or the fish of their choice) and a small bag of plain potato crisps. (Avoid fancy flavours in crisps, especially anything involving sweet chilli.)

Drinks are easy. Fill drink bottles with water and freeze them. If children don't want water, they're not thirsty. The temperature is far more important than the taste to a hot and bothered schoolkid.

Yoghurt and yoghurt-like snacks (often called 'dairy treats' or 'dairy snacks') are not an option for the lunchbox or for home. They are invariably very high in sugar (otherwise most kids wouldn't touch them, as yoghurt is intrinsically sour). Unfortunately, there isn't a low-sugar option available in this type of food unless you want to stray into artificial sweeteners, and I don't recommend these for anything other than getting through the withdrawal period (see chapter 4). The same thing applies to stewed-fruit snacks; they are usually served in a fruit syrup and have a significant proportion of the fibre removed because they are peeled. If fruit is what your children want, give them fresh fruit or frozen berries.

For extra snacks, cracker biscuits (our kids like BBQ Shapes) or nuts (presuming nuts are allowed at your school – check first) are fine. These are also great to have on hand when the starving hordes descend on your cupboards after school. Kids in search of afternoon snacks will eat anything that is not nailed down, so it's important to ensure your cupboards contain only sugar-free options. Crackers and nuts are great because most kids view them as a treat and neither contains appreciable amounts of fructose. Beware, though, that as your children's appetite control returns to normal, filling up at afternoon tea will mean they don't feel much like eating dinner (no matter how fabulous a cook you are).

School tuckshops

In recent years, most school tuckshops have become 'healthy' due to government regulations aimed at doing something about obesity. Unfortunately, the definition of 'healthy' leaves much to be desired from a sugar-free perspective. There is nothing wrong with a meat pie or a sausage roll but they have been deleted from most tuckshop menus and often replaced by salads and rolls drenched in commercial mayonnaise (or, even worse, fat-free mayo). Sugary soft drinks are no longer on the menu, but children are being to encouraged to drink fruit juice (which is often higher in sugar than the soft drink they've replaced) instead. In one school near me, the tuckshop has replaced soft drinks with sports water, because the water is 'only' 4.2 per cent sugar as opposed to the 11 per cent in most soft drinks. Unfortunately, the 8.4 g of sugar in the 200 ml bottle is *all* fructose – so one drink of sports water is the same as feeding a child four teaspoons of sugar. Bags of lollies are gone, but they've often been replaced by dried fruit (75 per cent sugar) and fruit muffins (45 g or 11 teaspoons of sugar per muffin, on average). So, there are possibly fewer low-sugar options available in the 'healthy' tuckshop than there were in the bad old days! See page 168 for some good tuckshop choices.

Party food

Kids like treats almost as much as the rest of us. Birthday parties and other special occasions require special foods. In the recipes in chapter 5, I've focused especially on this area. Birthday cakes, ice-creams, cupcakes and icing are necessary treats for kids. But they are impossible to find in a shop without vast amounts of sugar. I've included recipes for special occasions to ensure your kids have treats that look and taste just like everything their friends have. And if there is a favourite party food I haven't managed to replicate then go ahead and buy it; it's not like they're eating it every day.

Good things to select from the tuckshop menu	Bad things
Bacon and egg muffin	Raisin toast
Vegemite sandwiches or rolls	Jam or honey sandwiches or rolls
Ham, cheese or salad sandwiches or rolls	Sandwiches that involve mayo or sauce
Salad without dressing	Salad with dressing
Hot dog, meat pie or sausage roll (all without sauce)	Fruit salad
Baked potato (without mayo)	Yoghurts or ice-creams
Popcorn (unflavoured)	Pikelets or muffins
Water	Sports water or juice
Milk	Flavoured milk

The rules

Just to remind yourself, here is a summary of the rules for living a healthy, sugar-free life.

Don't eat sugar

1. Believe you are not being deprived *or*
   Have the right attitude (p. 42).
2. Do not snack on sugar (p. 46).
3. Once a sugarholic, always a sugarholic; you can't afford to have even a little (p. 89).
4. Don't concern yourself with fat content other than to steer clear of low-fat foods (p. 103).
5. Party food is for parties (p. 162).

4. WHAT ON EARTH IS THAT?
THE WORLD OF SUBSTITUTE SWEETENERS

As a recovering sugarholic, you are going to be drawn inexorably towards artificially sweetened foods. You will discover that your favourite yoghurt has a 'diet' option and it will seem like the easy way through withdrawal. Or you will (as I did) use artificially sweetened drinks as a crutch to break the habit you've associated with sugar consumption. And while artificially sweetened foods are excellent tools for getting through withdrawal, they are not a long-term solution. The good news is that by the end of withdrawal you will have lost your desire for sweet food altogether and are not likely to be consuming significant quantities of artificially sweetened food anyway. The bad news is that sometimes artificially sweetened is the only non-sugar option available.

I'm not a big fan of the term 'artificial sweetener'. It implies that other sweeteners (such as sugar, fruit juice or high-fructose corn syrup) are in some way natural, with all the goodness that term seems to suggest. But there is nothing natural about extract-ing sugar from sugar cane. (If you try chewing on a piece of sugar cane, you'll understand how much fibre you'd be getting if you ate it whole!)

'Substitute sweetener' strikes me as a more appropriate description than artificial sweetener. These substances are substitutes for sugar, intended to do the job of sugar. (In reality, sugar itself is a substitute sweetener – for honey – but let's not get all technical.) Substitute sweeteners are created using various levels of technology (from man-made beehives to industrial chemical plants) with the sole purpose of adding a sweet taste to foods that are not otherwise sweet. There are three categories of substitute sweetener as far as a recovering sugarholic is concerned: those that are absolutely safe to consume, those that may be safe in limited doses or over limited timeframes (your call), and those that are not safe under any circumstances.

Your call

A high-intensity sweetener is one that is several hundred to several thousand times sweeter than sugar. Our body can metabolise some

Safe	Your call	Unsafe	
Dextrose	Acesulphame	Agave syrup	Maltitol (#965)
Glucose	potassium (#950)	Corn syrup	Mannitol (#421)
Glucose syrup	Alitame (#956)	Fructose	Maple syrup
Lactose	Aspartame (#951)	Fruit juice extract	Molasses
Maltose	Aspartame-acesuphame	Golden syrup	Polydextrose
Maltodextrin	(#962)	High-fructose corn	Resistant dextrin
Maltodextrose	Cyclamates (#952)	syrup (HFCS)	Sorbitol (#420)
	Erythritol (#968)	Honey	Sucrose
	Neotame (#961)	Inulin	Wheat dextrin
	Saccharin (#954)	Isomalt (#953)	
	Stevia (#960)	Lactitol (#966)	
	Sucralose (#955)	Litesse	
	Xylitol (#967)		

Figure 4.1: Substitute sweeteners

of these but not others. Either way, it doesn't matter much because so little of them needs to be used (usually less than a tenth of a gram in a typical serving of soft drink). You are most likely to encounter this category of sweeteners in soft drinks and yoghurts, but you could find them anywhere. Most of them don't go by their technical name. They are usually listed on product packaging either as a brand name such as Splenda (for sucralose) or, more often, simply as a number, such as sweetener #951 (for aspartame). Artificial sweetener use has skyrocketed over the last two decades (see Figure 4.3). If it hadn't, the average American would be eating 21 kg per annum more sugar (10.5 kg more fructose)!

In *Sweet Poison*, I looked at the history of some of the primary sweeteners and pointed out that the science on their toxicity or otherwise was very much unproven. The current state of play is that all the sweeteners I discuss here are permitted in food in Australia and New Zealand, and you are likely to encounter them in artificially

Product	#950 Ace K	#951 Aspartame	#952 Cyclamate	#954 Saccharin	#955 Sucralose	Sugar alcohols
Fruit in jelly or syrup			✓	✓		
Chewing gum and mints	✓	✓				✓
Most diet soft drinks	✓	✓			Occasionally	
Pepsi Light and Diet Coke		✓				
Energy drinks	✓				✓	
Yoghurts	✓	✓			Occasionally	
Ice-cream	✓				✓	✓

Figure 4.2: Common low-calorie foods and the sweeteners generally used

sweetened foods. When I was in withdrawal, I decided that I was prepared to risk any potential downside of using these sweeteners so I could break the habits I had built around consuming sugar. I figured 3–4 weeks probably wouldn't kill me, and so far I've been right (touch wood).

However, since the publication of *Sweet Poison*, some interesting new research has been undertaken to find out whether or not people who consume these chemicals are actually healthier. And the answers that are coming back are not what the beverage industry wants to hear. Diet soft drink in particular is a massively accelerating market. High-intensity sweeteners now account for 5 per cent of the sweetener market when measured in terms of the amount of sugar (or HFCS) they are replacing. And it stands to reason: with four in five of us overweight or obese, we're all trying to do whatever

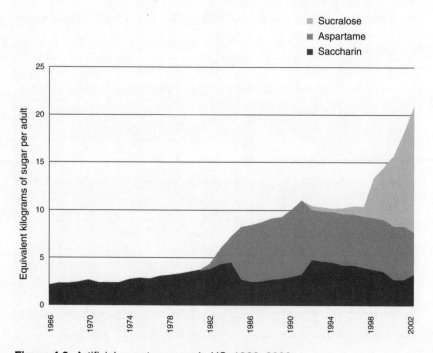

Figure 4.3: Artificial sweetener use in US, 1966–2002

we can to reduce weight. Diet soft drink surely can't hurt? Well, some of the latest research is suggesting that it can hurt, and the aspartame-causes-cancer rumour (for which I can find no reliable evidence) is perhaps the least of our concerns regarding high-intensity sweeteners.

Three major population studies have now been completed looking at the issue of diet soft drink consumption and whether it does any harm. The studies were done because at least eight significant studies conducted from 1989 to 2002 concluded that people who ate and drank low-calorie foods were no thinner than the rest of us. Yep, apparently it's true: drinking and eating artificially sweetened products does not make you thinner than you would have been had you just stuck to the full-strength version.

These three population studies take the results of health and lifestyle questionnaires completed over a number of years and perform statistical analysis on the answers. You don't have to be Einstein to see that this is not scientifically rigorous. There is no control group and there are enormous numbers of complicating factors that could be in play. But it is possible to eliminate many of those factors and whilst you wouldn't take the results to the bank, when significant correlations come up, they are good signposts for more detailed work.

The most recent study looked at a database of 6814 mixed-race Americans. The questionnaire was issued to the participants four times over an eight-year period (2000–2007). Over each questionnaire cycle, the participants were followed up with three physical examinations. The questionnaire was designed to (amongst many other things) identify the number of diet soft drinks the person consumed per day. The results make for interesting reading indeed. As expected, drinking more diet soft drinks did not lead to any of the participants being thinner than their counterparts who were drinking full-sugar drinks. But of far more concern was the fact that their risk of type 2 diabetes was not reduced either. Drinking one can (or more) of diet soft drink per day increased a person's risk of type 2 diabetes by 67 per cent (which is about the same increase as for someone drinking a can or more of full-sugar soft drink per day).

The diet soft drinkers did not have any particular increase in risk for the other markers of fructose consumption (blood pressure, heart disease or stroke) but in terms of weight (particularly central adiposity or tummy fat – the most dangerous kind) and type 2 diabetes, they were no better off than people drinking sugar-sweetened drinks. The researchers had no control over what sweetener was being consumed; in all probability it was a mix of the various types used in soft drinks as a general rule (aspartame, sucralose and saccharin). And since this was an observational study, they could not be sure what caused the outcome. There are all manner of theories that range from psychology to hormonal biochemistry, but the reality is that at this stage nobody has definitively proven anything. The upshot is that all or some of the sweeteners used to replace sugar in soft drinks are likely to make us just as fat and just as likely to contract diabetes as the sugar does. On the upside, consuming them instead of sugar will reduce the amount of fat in your arteries, and generally reduce your likelihood of dying of heart disease and stroke – but then again, water would do the same, and take care of the weight and the diabetes as well.

Clearly, more studies are needed – the kind of studies where we use controls, or people who are not using the product, alongside people who are. We need studies that can help us to nail down whether all sweeteners cause weight gain and increased risk of type 2 diabetes (which would perhaps point to a psychological rather than a chemical problem) or whether it is one (or more) of them in particular.

The primary high-intensity sweeteners

Saccharin (sweetener **#954**), the oldest high-intensity sweetener, was accidentally discovered in 1878 by scientists working on coal-tar derivatives at the John Hopkins University in the United States. It is marketed under the brands 'Sweet'N Low' and 'Sugar Twin'. Saccharin is banned in Canada but is permitted in Australia. It is about 300 times as sweet as sugar but has an unpleasant metallic aftertaste that limited its potential market to people who really had no choice (diabetics). But in 1937, a partial solution was discovered: cyclamate.

Cyclamate (sweetener **#952**) is much less sweet than saccharin, at only 50 times as sweet as sugar. It also has an unpleasant aftertaste, but less so than saccharin and, to some extent, when they are mixed together they mask each other's aftertaste. Saccharin mixed with cyclamate (10 parts cyclamate to one part saccharin) was marketed as a sugar substitute in restaurants under the brand 'Sweet'N Low' and was used in the first no-calorie soft drink, 'TaB', released by Coca-Cola in 1963. Cyclamate is now banned in the United States but is permitted in Australia. Cyclamate and saccharin had the market to themselves until 1981, when aspartame (aspartyl-phenylalanine) received US Food and Drug Administration approval.

Aspartame (sweetener **#951**) tastes similar to sugar and has the same number of calories. It is, however, 200 times sweeter, so where a soft-drink manufacturer would use 40 g of sugar in a can, they can replace it (and its 220 calories) with less than one quarter of a gram of aspartame, which provides just one calorie. Unlike cyclamate and saccharin, aspartame is actually digested by the body rather than passing straight through. Aspartame is marketed as 'Nutrasweet' and 'Equal', and is the sweetener used most commonly in diet soft drinks. I ingested large quantities of it while getting unhooked from high-sugar soft drinks.

Alitame (sweetener **#956**) and **neotame** (sweetener **#961**) were developed in the early 1980s. Like aspartame, they are based on aspartic acid, a chemical building block for various plant proteins. Alitame is 2000 times sweeter than sugar and about 10 times as sweet as its big brother, aspartame. Neotame is up to 13000 times sweeter than sugar. Neither alitame nor neotame is as stable (when cooked) as aspartame, but unlike aspartame, they don't produce phenylalanine when digested, which means the label doesn't need to carry warnings for people with phenylketonuria. Alitame is approved for use in China, Australia and New Zealand but not in the US. Neotame was approved for use in the US in 2002 and is also approved in Australia and New Zealand.

Sucralose or **trichlorogalactosucrose** (sweetener **#955**) is chlorinated sugar – hence the marketing spin that it is made from sugar. (Technically it is, but by the time they've finished with it, it is no more sugar than, say, wood or another carbohydrate.) It tastes 600 times sweeter than sugar. Sucralose is marketed as 'Splenda' and was approved for use in Australia in 1993 and the US in 1998. Like aspartame, sucralose has the same number of calories as sugar and is digested by our bodies. However, being three times as sweet as aspartame, even less of it needs to be used to obtain the same effect. Sucralose is also used in soft drinks but is used most often in low-calorie foods, where its sugar-like characteristics (when cooked) make it most handy.

Acesulfame potassium (sweetener **#950**), sometimes called **Ace K**, is considered a great blending sweetener that helps improve the flavour of other low-calorie sweeteners. It was first used in soft drinks in 1998, but its biggest success is its combination with aspartame in just about everything.

Some testing has already begun in the hunt for an answer to the sweeteners/weight gain question. Susan Swithers and Terry Davidson at Purdue University in Indiana have been doing some rat experiments that compare rats fed glucose-sweetened yoghurt with rats fed saccharin-sweetened yoghurt. Susan and Terry are behavioural psychologists and they are trying to determine whether the observed weight increases associated with high-intensity sweeteners have a behavioural source. Their theory is that we (or at least rats) are evolved to associate sweet taste with energy. And that as a result, when we taste sweetness, a chain of physiological responses are set off that regulate how much we eat and how much energy we expend. If we fool around with that association by eating food that tastes sweet without expending the associated energy, then those associations will get all out of whack and the result will be that we overcompensate by eating more and exercising less. In other words, the sweet taste gets us ready to use energy: insulin is released in preparation for disposing of the blood glucose and a range of other hormones get ready to dispose of the fuel. When the fuel is not forthcoming, those links between the taste and the response are destroyed, so that a sweet taste does not generate the expected rush of appropriate hormones. This means not so much that the sweetener makes you fat but that the normal food does because you are not prepared for the digestion.

Going by the population studies I mention above, you'd expect both groups of rats in this study to put on weight. But Susan and Terry were comparing a sweetener to glucose and not to the glucose/fructose combinations used to sweeten full-strength soft drinks (HFCS in the US and sugar here). The population studies showed that full-strength and diet soft drinkers both put on weight at the same rate. In the rat study, the saccharin-eating rats piled on the weight, but the glucose eaters did not (other than as a growing rat would naturally). However, the saccharine group was eating about the same amount of yoghurt as the glucose group. So, it seems that the reason the saccharine group was becoming fatter than the glucose group was that they were eating more of everything else (both groups had unlimited access to rat food as well as the yoghurt), *not* because they were eating more of the thing they thought was sweet. The researchers also noticed that the glucose-fed rats were a bit more active than the saccharin-fed rats.

The researchers felt that these results backed up their theory of psychological disconnects leading to hormonal imbalances, but they were quick to say that it was difficult to be certain. Personally, I struggle with this theory and I don't think the study proves it in any convincing way, but it does provide some interesting insights on what happens when you compare rats fed glucose with rats fed saccharin. And it's about as accurate and recent as the research in this area gets.

Stevia (sweetener #960)

Stevia was not in circulation in the US when the studies linking high-intensity sweeteners to diabetes were being done, so there's no way of knowing whether it would have the same result. If the link is psychological then the answer is probably yes. But if it's chemical then the answer may be different.

Stevia is shorthand for a plant called *Stevia rebaudiana*, a relative of the sunflower and native to South and Central America. *Stevia* leaves contain stevioside (300 times as sweet as sugar) and rebaudioside (450 times as sweet as sugar). The plant makes stevioside and rebaudioside by joining two molecules of glucose to a molecule of steviol. The extreme sweetness comes from the steviol; the rest is just glucose. So, from a fructose perspective, there's nothing wrong with stevia – there ain't no fructose there. The big question is whether eating large quantities of steviol has any detrimental effects. Japan has used stevia as its main non-sugar sweetener (including in Diet Coke) for more than 30 years. It has been approved for use in Australia and New Zealand since 2008, and the studies done universally suggest it is safe in the quantities we are likely to consume.

My only lingering concern about stevia is that researchers don't really know what the human body does with the steviol. They know it has some effects (which they don't consider to be significant) on insulin and blood glucose levels. The overall impression I gained from reading these reports and studies was similar to the one I expressed in *Sweet Poison* concerning artificial sweeteners: they seem safe but they haven't been in our diet long enough to be sure. Check back in 30 years. Would I eat a product sweetened with stevia? Probably, if I really needed a sweet hit, but I wouldn't make a habit of it.

For a recovering sugarholic, the answer to the sweeteners/weight gain question is reasonably clear (until proven otherwise). High-intensity sweeteners do not appear (on their own) to make you less fat. And it seems likely they will not reduce your risk of type 2 diabetes. They are less deadly than fructose in that they do not fill your arteries with fat and, critically, they do not appear to produce a cortisol response. Since the cortisol response is likely to be at least part of the reason why fructose is addictive, these sweeteners can be used to break the addiction by substituting for sugar in the habits you have developed around your addiction. However, they are not a long-term substitute.

Whenever you can, substitute glucose-sweetened foods for sugar-sweetened ones rather than using artificial sweeteners. When you can't (and I suspect that until a sugar-free lifestyle becomes an awful lot more popular, there will be some times when you can't), then use these sweeteners to break the addiction. Always bear in mind, however, that high-intensity sweeteners are not a lifelong choice. You will still be doing significant damage (weight gain and diabetes, that we know of) until you give them up. But at least you will be breaking the sugar addiction. The good news is that after you've broken your addiction, these products will not seem worth the aftertaste and you will probably stop consuming them by choice.

Unsafe

One of the things likely to tempt you during withdrawal (if you are anywhere near a shop) will be sugar-free gum and those little packets of sugar-free mints they put next to the checkout. You know the sort of thing: Kopiko, Licorette, Extra and Jols, to name a few. They're sold on being great for your teeth, great for your breath and, to top it off, they contain no sugar. What more could you want?

Instead of sugar, they contain the following goodies:

Product	Sweeteners
Airwaves	isomalt, sorbitol, mannitol, Ace K, aspartame
Eclipse gum	sorbitol, maltitol, mannitol, Ace K, aspartame
Eclipse mints	sorbitol, Ace K, sucralose
Extra for Kids	sorbitol, xylitol, mannitol, Ace K, alitame
Extra Liquid Drops	isomalt, xylitol, Ace K, aspartame
Extra Professional	sorbitol, xylitol, mannitol, Ace K, aspartame
Extra Tab	sorbitol, mannitol, Ace K, aspartame
Extra Whitening	sorbitol, maltitol, mannitol, Ace K, aspartame
Jols	sorbitol, maltitol, Ace K, aspartame
Kopiko	isomalt, maltitol
Licorette	sorbitol, maltitol, Ace K, aspartame
Sassy	sorbitol, mannitol, Ace K, aspartame
Well Naturally chocolate	polydextrose, erythritol, sucralose
Cadbury Lite chocolate	isomalt, polydextrose, aspartame

· There are two main types of sweetener being used in this lot. The high-intensity sweeteners (Ace K, aspartame, alitame and sucralose) that I discussed above, and a range of sugar alcohols (sorbitol, isomalt, mannitol, maltitol).

Sugar alcohols

Sugar alcohols (also called polyols) are chemical derivatives of sugar that differ from their parent compounds because they have an alcohol group (in other words, they are part alcohol, part sugar). For example, mannitol is the sugar alcohol of fructose and maltitol is the sugar alcohol of maltose. In sugar-free gum and other similar items, sugar alcohols are the dominant sweetener, largely because of their bulk. They take up just as much space as sugar and behave like sugar. The 'foods' they imitate are almost 90 per cent sugar (and rubber, in the case of gum) so sugar alcohols need to be like sugar in the way they work.

As a group, sugar alcohols are not as sweet as sugar but they generally have about half the calories. This is not because they are inherently low-calorie, but because we simply cannot digest more than one-half to two-thirds of a sugar alcohol. So, for example, about 65 per cent of the sorbitol you eat makes it into your bloodstream. The other 35 per cent feeds the bacteria in the large intestine, resulting in diarrhoea and gas. This is why it is sometimes an important ingredient in 'natural' laxatives and why many products containing sugar alcohols bear a warning about a potential 'laxative effect'. The lack of sweetness in sugar alcohols is the reason these products also contain high-intensity sweeteners. Sugar alcohols also mask the aftertaste of those sweeteners and have a noticeable cooling sensation when they hit your tongue, which is great for mint-type products. The sugar alcohols are there for bulk, cooling and masking, but with fewer calories. The other sweeteners are there for their sweet taste. So, these little products at the checkout might not look like much, but each is a triumph of modern chemistry, and not necessarily something you want to consume.

The common sugar alcohols

Sorbitol (sweetener **#420**) is half as sweet as sugar. The 65 per cent of it that makes it into your bloodstream is immediately metabolised to fructose by your liver. Sorbitol is often the sweetener of choice in 'sugar-free' cough syrup. Sorbitol is also often sold as a laxative and, even in small amounts, can aggravate irritable bowel syndrome. It works (as a laxative) by sucking water into the large intestine. This has the effect of stimulating bowel movements.

Isomalt (sweetener **#953**) is half as sweet as sugar. It consists of two molecules of glucose joined to a molecule of sorbitol and a molecule of mannitol. Both the sorbitol and the mannitol are metabolised to fructose.

Mannitol (sweetener **#421** – sometimes called **manna sugar**) is half as sweet as sugar. It is the sugar alcohol of fructose and is metabolised as if it were fructose.

Lactitol (sweetener **#966**) is 40 per cent as sweet as sugar and does not occur naturally. It is a man-made sugar alcohol of lactose. Unlike all the others, lactitol is not absorbed at all by our digestive systems. Instead, it feeds the bacteria in our large intestine and in this way acts in almost identical fashion to inulin and polydextrose (see page 185), in that it pumps fatty acids into our bloodstream via absorption from the large intestine.

Maltitol (sweetener **#965**) tastes almost as sweet as sugar and is metabolised to glucose and sorbitol. Unlike the other sugar alcohols, maltitol doesn't have any real cooling effect.

When you see sorbitol on a label, your body sees fructose (well, 65% fructose, anyway). When you see maltitol, your body sees glucose (50%) and fructose (50%). This is just like sugar only slightly less of it gets absorbed. And with maltitol, you have the added benefit of wind-pain (if you eat more than 10–20 g of the stuff per day). When you see isomalt on a label, your body sees glucose (50%), fructose from sorbitol (25%) and fructose (25%). Again, just like sugar. Sure, these products (and many more like them) all have fewer calories than products containing equivalent quantities of sugar. They achieve this because less of the sugar substitute makes it into your bloodstream. But if fructose is what you are trying to avoid, you might as well be eating sugar for all you are achieving by eating these. You could get the same effect by cutting the full-sugar version in half and sticky-taping on half a laxative pill (perhaps a bit of an exaggeration, but you get the idea). Recovering sugarholics should avoid products containing sorbitol, isomalt, maltitol and mannitol. Because these products are metabolised to fructose anyway, you are not doing anything towards breaking your addiction by eating them.

Safe sugar alcohols

Erythritol and xylitol are exceptions to my advice to avoid sugar alcohols. Erythritol is comprehensively ignored by all of our potential digestion routes and passes straight through. That said, testing is fairly thin on the ground and I guess I have a natural aversion to eating things that seem too good to be true. Nevertheless, the science that has been done would appear to indicate that erythritol is not going to hurt you the way fructose will, or in any other way (that we currently know of). There also doesn't appear to be a whole lot to complain about with xylitol (aside from the price and the pet-unfriendly aspects – see box, pages 184–5). Even so, I doubt

I'll bother. Glucose costs a tenth as much and triggers all of our appetite controls.

Erythritol and xylitol

Erythritol (sweetener **#968**) is a sugar alcohol fermented from glucose. Like other sugar alcohols, it is about half as sweet as sugar, but unlike most of the rest, it has no calorific value. Studies on its metabolism show that about 90 per cent is absorbed by our small intestine and 10 per cent makes it into our large intestine. The 90 per cent is ignored by our liver and appears intact in our urine. The 10 per cent is ignored by our gut bacteria and appears in our faeces.

Xylitol (sweetener **#967**) is roughly as sweet as sugar but only has about two-thirds of the calories (because we only absorb two-thirds of it). So while it is a *lower* calorie sweetener, it's not particularly low-calorie. It's made by fermenting xylose, a sugar found in the embryos of most edible plants. The bacteria in your mouth responsible for tooth decay are not big fans of xylitol. It has been shown to significantly slow their growth and, as a result, is often used in chewing gums that proclaim their decay-fighting properties. But xylitol costs about ten times as much as regular sugar and this limits its commercial use.

Our livers rapidly convert xylitol back to xyulose and then glucose, so from the fructophobe's perspective, xylitol is ineffectively absorbed glucose. Because only two-thirds of it is absorbed, eating more than about 130 g of xylitol per day will give you diarrhoea, but other than that there don't appear to be any ill effects in humans. Dogs, however, are a different matter.

Recent studies show that dogs that eat more than 1 g of xylitol per kilo of body mass are in mortal danger of low blood sugar (leading to death) or liver failure (yep, death again). The results cannot be replicated in rats, horses, rhesus monkeys or humans (I bet there weren't too many volunteers for that trial), but it's a warning to keep the sugar-free gum away from Spot (if it contains xylitol). No testing has been done on cats, so unless you want Fluffy to be an interesting write-up in a science journal, it might be a good idea to keep it away from her as well.

Polydextrose, inulin and wheat dextrin

Plants convert sunlight to energy by creating sugars. The two primary sugar molecules are fructose and glucose. To store this energy, plants join these simple sugars together in long chains. Chains that are mostly glucose are called glucans. Polyxdextrose (sweetener #1200 – sometimes called Litesse) is a man-made glucan that is a long chain of glucose molecules with about 10 per cent sorbitol tacked on the end. Wheat dextrin is a similar man-mad chain of glucose molecules. Cellulose, the hard stringy indigestible bits of plants we usually call fibre, is also a glucan. Starch is another important glucan (the once most commonly encountered in our daily diet). It forms the foundation for most of the carbohydrates we eat. Animals (like us) also store energy as glucans. When we have too much glucose in our blood, we create glycogen (a glucan) and store it around our livers as a short-term supply of glucose (to get us through between antelope kills).

Polydextrose is increasingly being used alongside artificial sweeteners in 'sugar-free' foods. Unlike sugar alcohols, polydextrose is not sweet at all. Instead, it is used to add texture and bulk to food without adding sweetness. It is often used as a replacement for sugar, starch and fat in foods such as cakes, sweets, yoghurts and ice-creams. Food Standards Australia New Zealand (FSANZ) has agreed to allow polydextrose to be counted as a fibre rather than a sugar, and food manufacturers love it because of the marketing it enables them to do on their products' labels.

For example, an ice-cream manufacturer can replace a label that says 26.2 per cent sugar with one that says 8.7 per cent sugar plus 8.4 per cent fibre (and some artificial sweeteners – in this case, sorbitol, Ace K and sucralose). The one with the low sugar and the fibre is a much easier label to market than the other.

Ice-cream: standard vs no-sugar-added		
	Nestlé Peters Original Vanilla	Nestlé Peters No Sugar Added Vanilla
Sugars (including lactose)	26.2%	8.7%
Dietary fibre (polydextrose)	–	8.4%
Sorbitol	–	11.5%

Sugar chains that are mostly fructose are called fructans. (Nobody knows why some plants store their sugar as fructans and others as glucans but researchers speculate that, given the types of plants that do it, it might have something to do with drought-tolerance.) Fructans are most common in onions and other tubers like chicory but they are also in barley, wheat, artichokes and asparagus. They are present to some degree in about 15 per cent of plants. One fructan that you might have seen popping up on the ingredients list of some foods is inulin (sometimes called chicory, chicory extract, fructo-oligosaccharide or FOS). Inulin is a chain of about 60 fructose molecules and one glucose molecule.

Why marketers love fructans and glucans

Our bodies do not have the enzymes (chopping shears) necessary to cut up a fructan like inulin or a glucan like cellulose, wheat dextrin or polydextrose. We do have enzymes for sugar, fructose, glucose and starch, so when we eat those sugars, they get dealt with immediately in our small intestine. But when we eat inulin, wheat dextrin and polydextrose, they sail straight through our small intestine and become food for the bacteria that inhabit our large intestine. Lactitol is not a glucan or a fructan but it behaves in exactly the same way; we can't digest it, but our gut bacteria can.

The bacteria in our gut love fructans and glucans, chomping away furiously on them and converting them into fatty acids (which we then absorb into our blood stream) and gases (which we . . . well, you get the picture). Because feeding gut bacteria encourages them to multiply, inulin, wheat dextrin and polydextrose are sometimes described as prebiotics (because as we feed them, they increase the number of good bacteria in our gut). Prebiotics are different from probiotics (like Yakult), which are just bacteria in a bottle (for when you are running a bit low).

All of these things count as fibre rather than sugar on the label. This, combined with the fact they can be advertised as a prebiotic, makes the food they are used in sound much healthier. An example of a food that uses inulin in this way is Bakers Delight Hi-Fibre Lo-GI White Bread. Yoghurt manufacturers like Vaalia also use it because it allows them to lower the fat and sugar content (on the label, at least) without affecting the 'mouth feel'. Diet purveyors also like to use inulin, wheat dextrin and polydextrose because they have the useful property of masking the aftertaste of the artificial sweeteners, and the manufacturers can promote the product as being a healthy, fibre-rich prebiotic.

Inulin, wheat dextrin and polydextrose are full of sugar but our digestive systems can't get at it directly. Instead, our gut bacteria digest it for us. The fatty acids created by the bacteria eventually find their way into our bloodstream. And some of the latest research says that fatty acids released in this way do not trigger an appetite-suppressing response (unlike normal dietary fat, which does). The hormone that tells us when we've eaten enough fat (CCK) is triggered in our small intestine. But at the time that polydextrose, wheat dextrin and inulin go sailing through there, they are not fats; they are turned to fat and absorbed in our large intestine, where there is no CCK to detect the fat.

This means that by consuming foods containing these ingredients, we could just be skinning the cat another way. Whether bacteria fill our arteries with fatty acids (when we digest inulin, wheat dextrin and polydextrose) or our liver does the job (when we digest fructose) is probably beside the point if none of them triggers a hormonal response that suppresses our appetite. In addition to the obvious damage of (effectively) consuming unregulated fat, I'm not convinced that we know enough about inulin, wheat dextrin and polydextrose to be certain that their effect on our bodies is not just as bad as pure fructose. I'll be avoiding foods that contain them and I suggest that all recovering sugarholics do the same. This doesn't mean I'll be avoiding onion and asparagus – we are adapted to eat fructans in the small quantities contained in those foods (just as we are adapted to eat whole fruit). But I will be avoiding anything that includes lactitol, polydextrose, wheat dextrin, chicory, inulin, fructo-oligosaccharide (FOS), or gluco-oligosaccharide (GOS) on the label as an added ingredient, including many brands of bread and yoghurt.

Safe

The only sugars a recovering sugarholic can safely consume are glucose and galactose (which is metabolised to glucose). Glucose is a single molecule and, whilst you will find pure glucose powder in a chemistry lab, you won't find much of it on the supermarket shelves. Instead, it comes in a variety of guises with different names. Dextrose monohydrate is a powdered version of glucose sold in 1 kg bags (for about $3) in the home-brew section of your local supermarket. When I refer to dextrose in the recipe section, this is what I am talking about. It is one molecule of glucose joined to a water molecule.

The closest thing you will get to pure glucose (in most supermarkets) is glucose syrup. You'll find it in the cooking section next to the cocoa and the flavouring and colourings. Another variant of glucose and often used as a bulking agent in processed foods, it will appear on the label as maltodextrin or maltodextrose. It is a longer chain of glucose molecules (around 20) joined together. When it hits your saliva, it breaks down to maltose (two glucose molecules joined together) and is digested as if it were pure glucose. Maltodextrin is not sweet; in fact, it really doesn't have a taste at all, but manufacturers use it to bulk up foods that have had sugar removed and replaced with high-intensity sweeteners. A speck of sucralose (600 times sweeter than sugar) takes up a lot less space than the sugar it replaces, so you need something neutral to fill it out. Maltodextrin is perfect for the job.

Name	Number of glucose molecules
Glucose	1
Dextrose monohydrate	1
Maltose	2
Maltotriose	3
Maltodextrin or maltodextrose	~4–20
Polydextrose and wheat dextrin	~20–80
Starch and cellulose	1000s

Maltodextrin vs wheat dextrin

Maltodextrin is not to be confused with wheat dextrin. Wheat dextrin is also a long chain of glucose molecules but the chemical bonds are such that our digestive enzymes cannot chop it up. It is sometimes called 'resistant dextrin', 'resistant starch' or, even more confusingly, 'resistant maltodextrin'. The 'resistant' part of the name means it is resistant to our digestion. Anything with 'resistant' as part of its name is classified as a fibre, but for the reasons I explained above, it is to be avoided. On the other hand, maltodextrin (and maltose and maltotriose) is fine. The only caution is that it is often accompanied by a high-intensity sweetener that is probably less than good for you.

The only other sugar that should pass your lips is lactose (and then, of course, only if you are not lactose-intolerant). Lactose is a galactose molecule joined to a glucose molecule. The galactose molecule is metabolised to glucose by your liver and lactose is therefore essentially pure glucose.

5. RECIPES

This chapter provides recipes for many popular sugar-replacement foods to help get you unhooked. It is not how to make meals that are obviously sugar-free (like bacon and eggs); rather, it is a guide to making foods that can satisfy the habit-driven cravings you'll most likely experience when going through sugar withdrawal. These are also foods for you to use as special treats for the rest of your life.

I didn't develop these recipes. My cake-baking talents are restricted to opening the packet of flour. My wife, Lizzie, has been in charge of the kitchen on every recipe. She has cooked each of them dozens of times, trying different combinations and adjustments until we (and a random selection of guinea pigs) were happy with the end product. My role was as the (critically important) consumer of all cakes and desserts. It was hard work but someone had to battle through all that ice-cream and cake (okay, I had a little help from the kids). The notes included with each recipe are based on what Lizzie has told me along the way, just in case I give the impression that I know which end of an electric mixer to hold.

Lizzie is not a professional cook and I am not a professional taster. We are just an average family using a kitchen that is probably similar to yours. These recipes are not complex or fiddly for exactly that reason. If you are Jamie Oliver, then hopefully these basic recipes will provide a great starting point for further experimentation using cured vanilla beans from the Peruvian hinterland.

Some important notes about dextrose

The dextrose that is referred to in most of the recipes is dextrose monohydrate. You can buy it in 1 kg bags from the home-brew section of your local supermarket (for about $3). It is pure glucose. Do not be confused by something called 'brewing sugar' (often stacked next to it), which is about 75 per cent sugar. If your supermarket doesn't have dextrose, ask for it; they can easily get it in. Dextrose looks like caster sugar but it's only a little bit sweet and it fizzes slightly on the tongue. (It reminds me of the lemon sherbet powder I used to consume on my way home from school.) It will taste sweeter and sweeter the further you get into withdrawal. If you taste it while you are still addicted to sugar (go on, dive in – you know you want to!), it will taste almost flour-like, but once you are a month or two past your addiction, it will taste almost as sweet as you remember sugar tasting.

Dextrose weighs about half as much as sugar, but it takes up more fluid than the equivalent amount of sugar and seems to burn at a lower temperature. Most of these recipes started life as a normal sugar-based recipe. In substituting dextrose, Lizzie generally (but not always) increased the wet ingredients (or decreased the dry ingredients, including the dextrose) until the end product tasted like we remembered the sugar version tasting. For good measure, we kept a stable of tame sugarholics on tap to try out the end result. Some recipes (such as the ice-creams and the meringues) would fool any sugar addict. Others (that tasted very sweet to us) were declared bland in comparison to the full-sugar version. I've highlighted any feedback we've got for each recipe.

Ingredient	Weight of 1 cup (g)
Sugar	250
Caster sugar	220
Dextrose monohydrate	135

Dextrose also affects the shelf-life of the end product if it is a dry food (like cakes and biscuits). A dextrose-based cake will not last as long as its sugar equivalent and most are best eaten within a day of making them. When fresh, they are scrumptious, but after a day or two at room temperature, they seem to become too moist and a little sticky. (They last longer in the fridge.) The bikkies last a little longer and can be used in school lunches for at least a week.

Finally, remember the warning from page 64:

Do not eat foods sweetened with dextrose (glucose) until you have completed withdrawal from sugar.

It is only once you remove fructose from your diet that dextrose (glucose) becomes a viable alternative to sugar. Consuming it while you still have fructose wreaking havoc with your appetite control, circulating fats and hormone levels will not help you and may well harm you. So, if you are going cold turkey with sugar, you can begin using these recipes right away; if you've decided on a gradual withdrawal, you'll have to wait.

A note about common ingredients and ovens

- When a recipe says 'cream', we use thickened cream. This doesn't necessarily mean that ordinary cream won't work just as well. But we know the recipe works well with thickened cream.
- When a recipe says 'eggs', we use extra-large (at least 59 g) eggs. Because dextrose sucks up any moisture, it's important to use bigger rather than smaller eggs.
- When a recipe says 'butter', we use salted butter. The recipes may taste sweeter if you use unsalted butter instead.
- When a recipe calls for vanilla essence, we don't specify a quantity because how much you use depends on your personal taste. Generally, half to one teaspoon (maximum) gives a good result.
- Most of the oven temperatures in these recipes are altered from their sugar-based originals, but you may find that your oven does better if you reduce either the temperature or the time.
- The oven temperatures are for a non-fan-forced oven. If your oven is fan-forced, drop the temperatures by 20°C.

Warning! You can still get fat eating dextrose.

You can force yourself to eat more than you need. If you get carried away with making some of these excellent recipes, you might find yourself with a constant supply of dextrose-based snacks. You will eat them and then later you will eat a meal. You will struggle to finish the meal because you are full of yummy cake, but you might push through. If that becomes a regular habit, you will put on weight. These recipes are for special occasions and for guests. You can have them without getting re-addicted or suffering any of the other ill effects of fructose consumption, but that does not mean you can stop listening to your appetite control system. If you eat half a cheesecake for afternoon tea, your appetite control will not tell you to eat again until (probably) lunchtime the next day. Listen to it or you will gain weight.

Ice-cream and icy-poles

When I started breaking my sugar addiction, I didn't have the benefit of a nice book like this one. I muddled through, reading labels carefully and eventually eliminating almost all sugar from the household. One thing I could not replace was ice-cream. There simply isn't a low-sugar version that doesn't also contain other things I'd prefer my family didn't eat regularly. I didn't mind not having ice-cream that much, but for the kids, it was a different matter. I initially solved the problem by implementing a rule of only one ice-cream dessert a week. Lizzie and I attached it to the hardest-sell meal (which at that time was curry). We figured limiting ice-cream was better than eliminating it (and making it seem even more appealing). Then, one day, one of the kids decided they wanted a sugar-free birthday cake. Lizzie was able to manage that pretty easily, but sugar-free icing eluded her, so she decided to give homemade ice-cream (with dextrose) a go. We didn't own an ice-cream maker so the result was a somewhat icy affair – so much so that the relatives who had to endure it gave us an ice-cream maker for Christmas! We now use that machine at least once a week. (The recipes still work without the churner, but the Vanilla Ice-cream comes out a little icy and the Chocolate Ice-cream comes out more like gelato). The rule is still only one ice-cream dessert a week, but now the ice-cream is sugar-free as well.

Ice-cream

There are loads of ice-cream recipes available and most of them will work well if you substitute dextrose for sugar (usually in about the ratio of 2 dextrose: 1 sugar). Most of the recipes call for egg yolks to make the base custard, which is a big waste unless you are making an awful lot of meringues (to use the whites). The Old-fashioned Vanilla Ice-cream recipe here uses whole eggs and the Chocolate Ice-cream doesn't use eggs at all, so they aren't nearly as wasteful.

About vanilla . . .

Vanilla is not always sugar-free.

Vanilla beans are not fructose-free. The whole beans, which come from the vanilla orchid, are about 13 per cent sugar by weight.

Natural vanilla extract is primarily sugar with some vanilla essence. It is sold for use in high-temperature recipes. You will not need it for any of the recipes in this book.

Imitation vanilla essence does not contain sugar. It is simply the active ingredient vanillan mixed with alcohol.

Natural vanilla essence is made by soaking vanilla beans in alcohol, which dilutes the sugar. Most manufacturers of commercial natural vanilla essence add sugar to bring the concentration back up to around 13 per cent. If you make it yourself (by storing three split vanilla beans in a cup of vodka sealed in a jar for two months), the sugar will be diluted to about 8 per cent.

Lizzie uses Queen Natural Vanilla Essence. One teaspoon contains 0.25 g of fructose, which is negligible. If you prefer to be completely sugar-free, use imitation vanilla essence.

Old-fashioned Vanilla Ice-cream

For a bit of variety, you can add flavouring (baking section of the supermarket) to this recipe or the Vanilla Ice-cream on page 198. Our kids like strawberry flavour, and strawberry essence doesn't contain sugar. Just add two tablespoons in place of the vanilla essence. Another nice variation is to add chocolate chips. The recipe for those is on page 218 (Chocolate Glaze).

Kids love an ice-cream even more if it's in a cone. The good news is that most ice-cream cones sold in the supermarket are very close to sugar-free. We use Betta Natural Cup Cones (less than 1 per cent sugar), but check the label.

Makes approx. 1.5 litres (with a churner, which adds air and volume)

1 cup dextrose
⅛ teaspoon salt
1¾ cups whole milk
2 large eggs, beaten in a large bowl
1½ cups thickened cream
vanilla essence

1. Mix dextrose, salt and milk in a saucepan and heat until steaming.
2. Whisk the hot mixture into the beaten eggs in the bowl, then return the mixture to the saucepan.
3. Heat the mixture for 3 minutes at a low–medium heat, stirring with a wooden spoon, until the mixture thickens. Don't let it boil as that will cook the eggs and curdle the mixture.
4. Pour the mixture back into the bowl, cover and refrigerate for an hour or two (until cold).
5. Stir in cream and vanilla essence.
6. Churn in an ice-cream maker until you have something the consistency of soft-serve ice-cream. Then put the mixture in an ice-cream container you've saved from your final shop-bought ice-cream purchase, and store in the freezer.

Vanilla Ice-cream (egg yolks only)

If you happen to be making meringues (see page 231) and end up with some leftover egg yolks, or you just prefer the taste of egg-yolk ice-cream (I do), then this is a useful recipe.

Makes approx. 1.5 litres

2 cups milk
1¼ cups dextrose
4 egg yolks
2 cups heavy thickened cream
vanilla essence

1. Combine milk, dextrose and egg yolks over a low heat (but don't let the mixture boil or it'll be sweet scrambled eggs).
2. Cook for 5–8 minutes, stirring constantly. The mixture will thicken slightly but will not coat the back of a spoon.
3. Chill the mixture in the fridge.
4. Stir in cream and vanilla essence.
5. Churn in an ice-cream maker and then freeze.

Chocolate Ice-cream

You can't get anything much simpler or more popular than this.

Makes approx. 1.5 litres

2 cups thickened cream
1 cup milk
1 cup dextrose
¼ cup cocoa
vanilla essence

1. Warm cream and milk in a saucepan.
2. Whisk together dextrose, cocoa and vanilla essence, then whisk this into the cream and milk.
3. Churn in an ice-cream maker and then freeze.

Chocolate Gelato

This recipe has a strong chocolate taste (which can be bitter). If it's not sweet enough, increase the amount of dextrose or reduce the amount of cocoa.

Makes approx. 750 ml

3 cups milk
¾ cup dextrose (or up to 1¼ cups, depending on your taste)
2 tablespoons cornflour
¾ cup cocoa

1. Whisk 1 cup of the milk with dextrose, cornflour and cocoa.
2. Put the rest of the milk on to boil.
3. Pour the boiled milk over the chocolate mixture and stir.
4. Return the mixture to a saucepan and stir over a low heat for 10 minutes or until it thickens.
5. Chill the mixture in the fridge.
6. Churn in an ice-cream maker and then freeze.

Icy-poles

We live in a sub-tropical climate and it doesn't hurt to be able to fish an icy-pole out of the freezer for the kids on a hot day. You will need icy-pole moulds for these recipes; we found them in a specialty kitchen shop.

Vanilla (Milk) Icy-pole

The sweetness of these icy-poles suits children who have been off sugar for a while, but we've found that even the neighbourhood kids (with sugar in their diets) like them.

Makes approx. 750 ml

1 tablespoon cornflour
2½ cups milk
½ cup dextrose
½ cup thickened cream
vanilla essence

1. Dissolve cornflour in ¼ cup of the milk and set it aside.

2. Bring the rest of milk to the boil.

3. Add the dextrose/cornflour mix to the boiling milk. Simmer for 4–5 minutes.

4. Remove from the heat and allow to cool to room temperature.

5. Stir in cream and vanilla essence.

6. Chill in the fridge (not you, the mixture).

7. Pour the mixture into icy-pole moulds and freeze for 12–24 hours before serving.

Orange (Water) Icy-poles

Orange flavour (essence) is stronger than other flavours. But you could try any of the essences in this recipe. They don't generally contain sugar and if by chance you find one that does, it will say so on the label, so always check.

Makes approx. 2 litres

2 litres water
1½ cups dextrose
1 tablespoon orange essence
food colouring (optional, but the icy-poles will look like plain ice if you don't add colouring)

1. Place all ingredients (except colouring) in a saucepan.

2. Heat the mixture gently to dissolve the dextrose.

3. Test the flavour and add more to taste if you wish.

4. Add colouring until mixture reaches the desired colour.

5. Pour into moulds and freeze for 12–24 hours before serving.

Savoury sauces

Some of our kids had a serious tomato-sauce addiction. For them, hash browns, chips and sausages were completely inedible without sauce. It's not hard to understand why they lusted after the stuff when you know it's around one-quarter sugar (and many brands are even more). We needed a replacement for tomato sauce that didn't contain sugar but which the kids would sign off on. One problem we had in replicating tomato sauce was that we had quite a few different brands in the cupboard and no two of them looked or tasted the same. Some were runny and light in colour but tasted sweet; some were thick and bright red but less sweet. In the end it was trial and error, but the mixture we came up with seems to satisfy the sauce addicts – although, interestingly, one of them decided to give up on sauce altogether if she couldn't have the real deal. Kids are adaptable and will choose from the available options. Once addiction is not part of the calculation, they choose based on flavour and (we have found) are often quite happy to just do without.

Tomato Sauce

This recipe produces a sauce which we think tastes similar to one of the commercial sauces we used to buy. But it is meant to be tweaked to your personal taste. Taste the sauce often as you are making it and vary the amount of dextrose and salt to your preference. In this recipe, the dextrose behaves like flour, thickening the mixture. If you add more dextrose, you might need to add in a bit of water to avoid producing something with the consistency of tomato paste.

Makes approx. 100 ml

125 ml passata (sieved tomatoes, available from the supermarket)
1 tablespoon dextrose
pinch of salt

1. Place passata in a saucepan over a medium heat and allow it to boil.
2. Lower the heat, then stir in the dextrose and add salt to taste.
3. When the mixture tastes right and is about the consistency you like (it will thicken when cooled), remove from heat, cool, bottle, and store in refrigerator.

Pizza Base (unsweetened scone dough)

This makes a great, almost totally fructose-free meal. I've included it here because it works well with the Tomato Sauce above.

2 cups self-raising flour
30 g butter
¾–1 cup milk
½ teaspoon salt

1. Preheat oven to 210°C (410°F). Grease a large baking tray.
2. Mix all ingredients together into a dough.
3. Pound, squish and fling dough around kitchen like your name's Mario.
4. When ready to top your pizza base, place it on the tray. Use a thin smear of tomato paste or some Tomato Sauce before topping with whatever you like from your sugar-free cupboards and fridge.
5. Bake for about 10 minutes (depending on topping).

Phillips Family Sugarless Ketchup

This recipe is for those of you with refined tastes (and a bit more time). I told a friend of mine about my struggles with sauce and, being a Canadian, he happened to have a recipe for homemade ketchup to hand. He decided to try modifying his recipe to see if it would work with dextrose. It most certainly does. I'm not much of a sauce fan (even when I was addicted to sugar), but even I use this tasty ketchup on the odd sausage roll.

All of the herbs used here have trace amounts of fructose but, given the relative concentrations – and the fact that they are full of fibre – it's not worth worrying about.

Makes approx. 1 litre

1 red onion, chopped
¼ fennel bulb, chopped (any more than ¼ bulb will overpower the flavour)
1 stick celery, chopped
small piece of ginger, sliced
2 cloves garlic, sliced
½ red chilli, finely chopped
bunch of basil, leaves picked and stalks finely chopped
1 teaspoon whole coriander seeds
2 cloves
olive oil
salt
pepper
3 × 400 ml tins chopped tomatoes (no sugar added, organic preferred)
200 ml red wine vinegar
¼ cup dextrose

1. Put vegetables, ginger, garlic, chilli, basil stalks (keep the leaves for later), coriander seeds and cloves in a large saucepan.
2. Add a good dash of olive oil, and salt and pepper to taste.
3. Gently soften over a low heat, stirring occasionally, for at least 15 minutes. Do not brown.
4. Add tomatoes and one tin of cold water.

5. Bring to the boil, then turn down the heat and simmer until the ketchup reduces by half (this could take up to 2 hours).

6. Whiz ketchup in a food processor with the basil leaves.

7. Sieve twice.

8. Place in a clean pan, adding the vinegar and dextrose.

9. Simmer until ketchup attains tomato-sauce consistency. Taste and add more salt and pepper if required.

10. Pour into sterilised bottles and store in a cool dark place (preferably the fridge, especially if you live north of Sydney). It will stay good for around six months.

Sugarless Coleslaw

Obviously, this is not a sauce recipe, but I've included it here because the sugarless version of coleslaw relies on the dressing used. Shop-bought coleslaw is full of sugar because of the mayonnaise used, but if you make your own salad and use whole-egg mayo, you'll be fine. Of course, you can add more things to the mix (like celery or capsicum), depending on your tastes.

Serves 4 (depending how much they like coleslaw)

1 large carrot
½ small cabbage (any type will do – the red ones add some nice colour)
1 apple (optional)
2–3 dessertspoons whole-egg mayonnaise

1. Finely chop carrot, cabbage and apple (if using), and mix together in a salad bowl.

2. Mix in mayonnaise, one spoonful at a time, until the coleslaw attains the level of gooiness you require. (Mixing is best done using your – or, even better, your children's – hands. They'll love it, and will be more likely to eat the end product, too.)

Simple Hollandaise Sauce

This sauce is great poured over freshly poached eggs.

Makes approx. 500 ml

4 egg yolks
1 tablespoon lemon juice
salt and white pepper to taste
250 g butter, melted and still warm

1. Place egg yolks, lemon juice, salt and pepper in the bowl of a food processor; process slowly for 30 seconds.
2. With the processor still running, slowly pour in butter and process until smooth.

Sweet sauces

If plain ice-cream isn't enough for you, here are some delicious sauces to drizzle over the top. The Caramel Sauce in particular is a cracker. But, like many things made with dextrose, these sauces won't last as long in the fridge as their sugar equivalents, so make them within a day or two of when you intend to use them.

Given you'll probably be taking a hatchet to your Christmas menu once you go sugar-free, it's nice to know that one staple of the festive season can remain. Warm custard can make even the blandest cake taste heavenly and, thankfully, custard recipes made with dextrose work beautifully. Our kids regard warm custard served with warm cakes or muffins as a real treat.

Caramel Sauce

Even serious sugar addicts are unable to tell the difference between this sauce and the sugary version.

Serves 4

1 cup dextrose
85 g butter
½ cup thickened cream

1. Heat dextrose in a saucepan on moderate heat. Stir vigorously with a whisk or wooden spoon as it melts.
2. Allow dextrose to boil. (If it burns, throw it out and start again, but next time add ½ cup water. Because the water has to evaporate before the dextrose will caramelise, it slows down the cooking and means that the dextrose cooks more evenly.)
3. As soon as the dextrose crystals have melted and coloured slightly, add butter and whisk until it is melted too.
4. Take the pan off the heat and count slowly to three.
5. Slowly add cream, whisking all the while, to incorporate.

(If the mixture starts to foam, slow down the rate at which you are adding the cream.)

6. Let the sauce cool for a few minutes, then pour into a glass jar. Remember that it is still very hot, so warm the glass with a little hot water before you start, to prevent breakage.

7. Store the sauce in the fridge but warm it up before serving.

Hot Fudge Sauce

This sauce is not overly sweet. If you are through withdrawal, you will love it. But if you have only just begun, it will taste slightly bitter in comparison to the full-sugar equivalent. Chocolate is a powerful and bitter flavour and it can overcome the weak sweetness of dextrose. You can add more dextrose to sweeten up this recipe, depending on what you intend to serve the sauce with. Ice-cream is pretty sweet and a less-sweet sauce will provide some tasty contrast, but cheese-cake, for example, is more bland and might require a sweeter sauce.

Serves 4

15 g butter
1 tablespoon cocoa
2 tablespoons dextrose (4 tablespoons if you prefer a sweeter sauce)
¼ cup thickened cream
½ teaspoon vanilla essence

1. Melt butter and cocoa over a low heat.

2. Add dextrose; stir to dissolve. (At this point, you could add more dextrose to sweeten up the sauce if you choose.)

3. Add cream and bring the mixture to the boil for 1 minute, stirring continuously.

4. Take the mixture off the heat; add vanilla essence and mix well.

5. The mixture will thicken as it cools. Store in the fridge but warm it up before serving.

Boiled Custard

This recipe is for people who can't bring themselves to waste vast quantities of egg whites (that would be me). If you're entertaining the Queen and wish to spare nothing in the effort, make the Egg Custard (opposite) instead.

Makes approx. 500 ml

1 tablespoon cornflour
600 ml milk
2 egg yolks
2–3 tablespoons dextrose (begin with 2 and add another at
    the end if necessary)
vanilla essence

1. Blend cornflour with a little of the milk.
2. In a separate bowl, beat egg yolks and dextrose with a little of the milk and set aside.
3. Place remaining milk in a saucepan and bring to boiling point.
4. Stir in the cornflour mixture and allow to boil for 2 minutes (continue stirring).
5. Remove the mixture from the heat and allow it to cool to room temperature.
6. Pour the cornflour mixture over the egg yolk mixture, beating well as you do.
7. Return mixture to pan and heat until it thickens enough to coat the back of a spoon. Do not let it boil or the egg yolks will cook.
8. Add vanilla essence.
9. Strain the custard (to remove any lumps) into a jug for serving.

Egg Custard

If you find yourself in possession of leftovers of this custard, it makes a delicious ice-cream. Based on about half the custard this recipe produces, add ½ cup thickened cream and ½ cup milk to the custard, then cool and churn in an ice-cream maker.

Serves 4–6

1 cup milk
1 cup thickened cream
1 vanilla bean
5 egg yolks
1 cup dextrose

1. Place milk, cream and vanilla bean (split) together in a saucepan and bring to a simmer.
2. Whisk egg yolks and dextrose until light and foamy.
3. Pour the milk and cream mixture into the egg yolks, whisking all the while.
4. Return the mixture to the stove over a moderate heat. Stir constantly until it thickens enough to coat the back of a spoon. (Do not let it boil.)
5. Strain to remove the vanilla bean and seeds (although if you are serving sophisticated guests, they won't mind the odd vanilla seed, and it does enhance the taste).
6. Serve the custard warm or cold (or, if you're unsophisticated, just drink it straight from the jug).

Cakes

It is important to remember, particularly with cake recipes, that dextrose takes up more fluid than sugar and bakes faster. When baking dextrose cakes, be careful not to overbeat the mixture (the dough will become tough) and watch the cake in the oven very carefully so that it does not burn.

After significant trial and error, Lizzie has finetuned the following cake recipes so that they work with dextrose. But there's nothing to stop you tinkering with your own sugar-based recipes. Just follow these rules:

1. Replace sugar for dextrose one for one (1 cup for 1 cup).
2. Increase the wet ingredients.
3. Use extra-large eggs or, if none is available, add an extra egg to the recipe.
4. Keep the beating to a minimum once any flour is added (or folded in).
5. Stay alert while the cake cooks (it may cook more quickly than you are used to). It may help to move your oven shelves further from the heat source.

Remember that these recipes will not produce overly sweet cakes for people who still eat sugar – especially the Chocolate Cake, because chocolate is bitter and can more easily overpower the weak sweetness of dextrose. But once you add dextrose icing or frosting, most people will struggle to tell the difference. If you are making a cake for a birthday party or some other celebration where sugarholics will be in abundance, you could use a sugar-based icing. By making the cake with dextrose, you have eliminated a significant quantity of fructose from the overall concoction. A sugarholic would not be able to tell the difference between the Chocolate

Cake here and a 'normal' chocolate cake if both were iced with sugar-based icing.

One piece of sugar-iced dextrose cake will not kill anyone (or re-addict them, either). For less celebratory eating, choose a dextrose-based icing. Be prepared to be flexible with celebrations and select the icing method that suits your cake – and the expectations of those who will be eating it. Remember, **party food is for parties** (see page 162).

It's also worth remembering that sugar is a preservative and dextrose isn't. Dextrose cakes last much better if kept in the fridge than if left on the bench (not that they even get a chance to cool if they are ready at about the time the kids get home from school). Dextrose-based doughs are much drier than sugar equivalents. Where you might normally pour a mixture into the baking tin, with most of these you will be using a spatula to ladle the dough out and spread it in the tin.

Chocolate Cake

A sugarholic might not like this cake much. But the further you get from being a sugarholic, the more you will love it. It is definitely a favourite with our kids, especially when iced with Mock Cream.

Makes 1 cake (which may serve anywhere between 1 and 300 people, depending on the generosity of the slicer)

1 cup self-raising flour
1 cup dextrose
3 tablespoons cocoa
2 eggs
½ cup milk
vanilla essence
55 g butter, softened

1. Preheat oven to 180°C (350°F). Grease and flour a 20 cm round cake tin.

2. Sift dry ingredients (flour, dextrose and cocoa) into an electric mixer bowl.

3. Add eggs, milk and vanilla essence.

4. Machine-mix until the mixture just comes together.

5. Add butter and beat the mixture for no more than 2 minutes.

6. Pour (or spread – this is quite a dry mixture) into the prepared tin.

7. Cook until a skewer inserted in the cake comes out clean (it should take about 50–60 minutes).

8. Remove from tin and cool on a wire rack.

9. Eat the cake plain or, if you prefer, ice with Mock Cream (see page 220).

Dextrose Cupcakes

The primary school our kids attend allows cake to brought on birthdays. All our kids take a box of these cupcakes iced with a dextrose icing (see page 218). The other kids in the class get into them with just as much gusto as they would sugar-based cupcakes.

Makes approx. 12

60 g butter
½ cup dextrose
vanilla essence
1 large egg
1 cup self-raising flour (scant)
pinch of salt
½ cup milk

1. Preheat oven to 180°C (350°F). Set out 12 patty pans.

2. Using an electric mixer, beat butter and dextrose to a cream.

3. Add vanilla essence and egg, and beat well.

4. In a separate bowl, sift together flour and salt.

5. Fold the flour and milk alternately into the butter/dextrose

mixture – you want the dough to be as soft as possible, so be gentle.

6. Spoon the mixture into patty pans.
7. Bake for approximately 15–20 mins or until firm to touch and just colouring.

Vanilla Cake

This is a great general-purpose cake. It makes a terrific base for birth-day cakes, especially if you top it off with the Mock Cream (of any flavour and colour) on page 220.

Makes 1 cake

150 g butter, softened
1 cup dextrose
2 large eggs
vanilla essence
⅔ cup milk
2 cups self-raising flour
pinch of salt

1. Preheat oven to 180°C (350°F). Grease and flour a block tin.
2. Using an electric mixer, beat butter and dextrose to a cream.
3. Add eggs, one at a time, beating well after each addition.
4. Add vanilla essence.
5. Sift together flour and salt in a separate bowl.
6. Fold one-third of the flour into the mixture, followed by half of the milk.
7. Continue adding the flour and the milk alternately until you have a soft dough (do not over-mix).
8. Spread evenly into the prepared tin.
9. Bake for approximately 40 minutes or until a skewer inserted into the cake comes out clean.
10. Remove from tin and cool on a wire rack.

Butter Cake

This cake, the Coconut Meringue Cake and the Cinnamon Teacake are all delicious without icing, which means less messing around before you get to the eating bit (my specialty).

Makes 1 cake

125 g butter, softened
1¼ cups dextrose
3 eggs
1 cup plain flour
½ cup self-raising flour
½ teaspoon baking powder
½ cup milk
vanilla essence

1. Preheat oven to 150°C (300°F). Grease and flour a 20 cm round cake tin.
2. Combine all ingredients in an electric mixer bowl and beat at low speed until just combined.
3. Beat at moderate speed for 1–2 minutes (no more) to make sure mixture is well combined. (If you overbeat, the cake will be too dense.)
4. Bake for about 1 hour (until a skewer inserted in the cake comes out clean).
5. Stand the cake for 5 minutes.
6. Turn out and rest cake right-side-up to cool.

Coconut Meringue Cake

This cake was a real surprise. It keeps very well (for a dextrose-based cake) and doesn't need icing. If you use shredded coconut instead of desiccated, it looks and tastes even more fancy.

Makes 1 cake

CAKE BASE
90 g butter
½ cup dextrose
3 egg yolks
vanilla essence
1 cup self-raising flour
½ cup milk

MERINGUE TOPPING
3 egg whites
¾ cup dextrose
1 cup desiccated coconut

Prepare cake base

1. Preheat oven to 180°C (350°F). Grease and line an 18 cm square cake tin.
2. Using an electric mixer, beat butter and dextrose to a cream.
3. Add egg yolks one at a time, beating well after each addition.
4. Add vanilla essence and beat again briefly.
5. Fold in one-third of the flour then half of the milk. Continue adding flour and milk alternately until complete and you have a soft mixture.
6. Turn into prepared tin.

Prepare meringue topping

1. Beat egg whites until stiff, then add dextrose, a little at a time.
2. Fold in coconut.
3. Spoon egg-white mixture over the cake mix in the tin.
4. Bake for approximately 40 minutes or until a skewer comes out clean.
5. Allow to stand for a few minutes before lifting cake out onto a wire rack to cool.

Cinnamon Teacake

There's nothing quite so civilised as a teacake. This recipe is great warm but doesn't keep very well. Whip it up just before you have guests over for elevenses.

Makes 1 cake

CAKE
80 g butter
pinch of salt
¾ cup dextrose
2 eggs, lightly beaten
1½ cups plain flour
1½ teaspoons baking powder
1 cup milk

TOPPING
1 tablespoon dextrose
1 teaspoon cinnamon powder
10 g butter

1. Preheat oven to 180°C (350°F). Grease and flour a 20 cm cake tin (Lizzie likes to use a ring tin).
2. Using an electric mixer, beat butter, salt and dextrose to a cream.
3. Add eggs and beat again to combine.
4. In a separate bowl, sift together flour and baking powder.
5. Fold in one-third of the flour then half of the milk. Continue adding flour and milk alternately until complete and you have a soft mixture.
6. Turn into prepared tin.
7. Bake for about 30 minutes (until a skewer inserted in the cake comes out clean).
8. For the topping, mix together dextrose and cinnamon powder.
9. Once the cake is cooked, and while it's still warm, spread the top with butter, then sprinkle over the topping.
10. Serve immediately.

David's Cinnamon Toast

If you're like me (pretty handy with the sprinkling but find the rest of the Cinnamon Teacake recipe somewhat of a challenge), try my variation here.

Serves 1 (David!)

1 tablespoon dextrose
1 teaspoon cinnamon powder
2 pieces of bread
10 g butter

1. Mix together dextrose and cinnamon powder in a small bowl.

2. Preheat toaster (i.e. switch it on).

3. Place bread in toaster.

4. Cook until golden brown.

5. Once cooked, and while it's still warm, spread toast with butter.

6. Sprinkle with cinnamon/dextrose mixture.

7. Serve immediately.

Icings

When it comes to icing, you have a choice. If you are after a particular 'look', you may find it hard to replicate using one of these recipes. So you could simply make your usual icing with icing sugar. If the look is less important and you wish to avoid the fructose altogether, try the Chocolate Glaze. Our kids would eat cupcakes covered in this stuff till the cows come home (mind you, they then wouldn't eat any dinner . . .).

Chocolate Glaze

Once this glaze has cooled a little, you can spread it on cakes. You can thicken it up by adding more dextrose. If it thickens too much, just put it back over the saucepan of hot water and warm it to melt the dextrose again. It dries to a hard, sweet and chocolatey finish that is especially good for cupcakes.

This glaze is also perfect if you want chocolate chips in your ice-cream. Rather than spreading the glaze on a cake, leave it in the fridge for a day, where it will harden into a sheet. Take it out and smash it up to your desired chip size, then chuck the chips into the ice-cream maker while your ice-cream is being churned. Scrumptious!

Makes enough to ice up to 24 cupcakes

2 tablespoons cocoa
3 tablespoons water
1 cup dextrose

1. Boil a saucepan of water and then turn off the heat.
2. Place cocoa and water into a smaller saucepan over a moderate heat and stir until it becomes a thick paste. Take the pan off the heat and stir in some of the dextrose.
3. Stand the saucepan containing the mixture over the saucepan of hot water (no longer boiling) on the stove to warm the mixture up again, but be careful not to boil it.
4. As the dextrose melts and combines with the cocoa mix, add

more dextrose, a little at a time, until all the dextrose is used.

5. Once all the dextrose is blended, take the saucepan off the heat, where the mixture will thicken and set.

Italian Buttercream Icing

This recipe uses egg whites only. Alternatives are French Buttercream (using egg yolks instead of whites) or American Buttercream (using whole eggs). The concern with each of these is that you don't cook the mixture much and you are using raw eggs. While the egg whites (in the Italian recipe) are mixed with hot dextrose syrup, it's certainly possible that the icing won't reach the 70°C (160°F) necessary to guarantee that any salmonella bacteria which may be present (in the egg) are destroyed. Make sure your eggs are fresh and have been refrigerated since you bought them. We have used this recipe quite a bit and haven't managed to kill anyone yet, but if you want to be absolutely certain, you could use powdered or pasteurised eggs (if you can get your hands on some).

Makes enough to ice one large cake (such as the Chocolate Cake or the Vanilla Cake)

¾ cup dextrose
1 tablespoon water
2 egg whites
pinch of cream of tartar
100 g butter
food colouring and/or flavouring of your choice

1. Heat dextrose and water in a saucepan over a moderate heat.

2. Allow the mixture to boil until it enters soft 'ball' stage (where a drop of mixture forms a ball when put in cold water).

3. Using an electric mixer, beat egg whites and cream of tartar to soft peaks.

4. Trickle the dextrose mixture into the egg whites while still beating, until combined.

5. Switch mixer bowls to beat the butter until light and fluffy.

6. Put the first bowl back and add the butter to the meringue mix a little at a time, beating constantly.

7. Add colour or flavour before icing cakes.

Mock Cream

Mock cream is a classic standby for cakes. It tastes particularly delicious on the Chocolate Cake. It doesn't work as well in a hot environment, so if you plan to use it, do so where it can be served from the fridge.

Makes enough to generously ice one large cake

125 g butter, softened (not melted)
1 teaspoon powdered gelatine
1 cup dextrose
¼ cup warm water

1. Using an electric mixer, beat softened butter until light and fluffy.

2. Sprinkle gelatine over two tablespoons of the warm water to soften.

3. Add dextrose to beaten butter and beat thoroughly until light and fluffy once again.

4. Add the gelatine mixture, a little at a time, beating well in between each addition.

5. It may be necessary to add the rest of the water to the mixture to improve the consistency. If you need to do this, do it slowly, one tablespoon at a time. Allow the mixture to absorb each addition before beating it back up to a fluffy consistency and then adding more if necessary. You are aiming for a mixture that is not grainy to taste. If you use up all of your ¼ cup and the mixture is still grainy, add up to another 2 tablespoons but no more. Too much water will drown this recipe and turn it into a gloopy mess that never sets.

6. Flavour and colour as desired.

7. Spread onto cakes, then refrigerate to set.

Muffins

All the muffin recipes are cooked in a mini-muffin tin, but a friand tin will work just as well. Anything bigger might overwhelm your guests – the Chocolate Brownies, in particular, are very dense. Remember to adjust the cooking time to suit the size of your tin (and, of course, keep a good eye on them in the oven).

Muffins are very flexible and forgiving. You can pretty much throw anything you like in the bowl. The other day Lizzie wanted to make Banana Muffins but had only one banana, so she topped up the mixture with frozen blueberries (fresh would also be fine). The resultant blueberry-banana muffins were a big hit. Once you've made the Banana Muffins, you'll get a feel for how runny the mixture should be. Then, if you want to experiment with other ingredients, just throttle the dextrose up or down to control the runniness (the more dextrose, the less runny the mixture). Blueberries tend to be more liquid and less sweet than bananas so you would need to double the amount of dextrose for blueberry muffins.

Remember that sugar is a preservative and these muffins will not keep like their sugar-based alternatives. But with kids who are not sugarholics, these will be inhaled so fast that you won't need to worry about storing them.

Chocolate Brownies

The Chocolate Glaze (see page 218), at its runniest, is great on these brownies. (The glaze sets and adds a layer of sweetness that is appreciated when they are served cold.) Just dip the tops of the brownies in a pot of the glaze. If you plan to serve them as a hot dessert, don't bother to glaze them, as they have such a delicious, dense, chocolatey flavour. For dessert, your only challenge is to decide whether ice-cream or custard will complement them best.

Makes approx. 24

150 g butter, softened (plus extra if needed)
1 cup dextrose
2 eggs
⅔ cup cocoa
1 cup self-raising flour

1. Preheat oven to 180°C (350°F). Grease two mini-muffin tins.

2. Cream butter and dextrose.

3. Add eggs.

4. Sift together cocoa and flour, and fold into butter mixture. The mixture should just come together; if it's too dry, add some extra melted butter.

5. Spoon into prepared tins (it's quite a dry mixture – you won't be pouring it).

6. Bake for 10–12 minutes until cooked but still soft in centre.

Banana Muffins

Obviously, this recipe is not fructose-free. The two bananas will contain approximately 10–12 grams of fructose (total). This means that each muffin will contain about one-third of a gram of fructose. But they will also contain the same fibre as in the banana. You would have to eat 20 of these muffins to get the same amount of fructose you'd get in one banana, so unless you plan not to share this batch with anyone, don't stress about the fructose content.

Makes approx. 40 mini-muffins

2½ cups self-raising flour
½ cup dextrose (although you can get away with as little as ¼ cup)
2 teaspoons baking powder
2 teaspoons ground cinnamon
2 eggs, lightly beaten
1½ cups milk
100 g melted butter
1 cup banana (2 medium bananas), mashed

1. Preheat oven to 190°C (375°F). Grease two mini-muffin tins.
2. Sift flour, dextrose, baking powder and cinnamon into a bowl, then make a well in the centre.
3. Combine eggs, milk and butter in a separate bowl, then pour the mixture into the well in the flour. Mix together with a wooden spoon.
4. Add mashed banana and mix until almost smooth.
5. Spoon into prepared tins. (You will probably need to bake these muffins in two batches, unless you have more tins and a very large oven.)
6. Bake for about 20 minutes or until golden brown.

Coconut Choc Muffins

These taste good just as they are but you can add a thin layer of sweetness by dipping the muffins tops in some Chocolate Glaze (see page 218).

Makes approx. 24

150 g butter
1 cup self-raising flour
1 cup dextrose
½ cup desiccated coconut
2 tablespoons cocoa
2 eggs, lightly beaten

1. Preheat oven to 180°C (350°F). Grease two mini-muffin tins.

2. Melt butter and leave to cool.

3. Mix dry ingredients together in a bowl.

4. In a separate bowl, combine butter and eggs; mix lightly.

5. Mix wet ingredients into dry.

6. Spoon mixture into muffin tins.

7. Bake for 10–15 minutes.

Biscuits and slices

Abandon any hope of making a biscuit like one you would buy in a packet from the supermarket. Those biscuits are hard (snappable) and very sweet; it is difficult to achieve either of these properties with dextrose. (The only really hard biscuit here is the Anzac Biscuit, which is snappable because it is made with glucose syrup rather than dextrose powder. That's a substitution you could try with other recipes if you're feeling experimental.)

Nevertheless, bikkies are important, if for no other reason than they are a quick and easy addition to a school lunch on a busy morning. Most of these recipes will produce biscuits that are of the softer variety (think shortbread). If you are used to Delta Creams or Monte Carlos, they will definitely be a comedown in terms of sweetness. But a few weeks out from withdrawal, they will really start to taste like a treat.

Chocolate Slice

Slices are so easy to make that the kids can help (no, I mean it – they really *can* help with this one). Just remember that when pouring over the Chocolate Glaze (which is runny), you will need a knife to ensure even coverage. Work quickly, before the glaze is absorbed by the slice. For best results, set and store in the fridge.

Makes approx. 16 slices

1¼ cups self-raising flour
2 tablespoons cocoa
¾ cup coconut
½ cup dextrose
160 g butter, melted and cooled
1 egg, lightly beaten

1. Preheat oven to 180°C (350°F). Line an 18 cm square shallow tin with baking paper.

2. Mix dry ingredients together in a bowl.

3. In a separate bowl, combine cooled butter and egg; mix lightly.

4. Mix wet ingredients into dry.

5. Press mix into prepared tin.

6. Bake for 10–15 minutes.

7. Cut into squares while still warm but leave in the tin to cool.

8. When cool, pour over a warm Chocolate Glaze (see page 218). Unlike the cupcakes, the warm glaze soaks into the upper layers of the warm slice and gives it a nice sweet finish.

Coconut Biscuits

This recipe makes a cake-like biscuit rather than the crisp hardness of the Anzac Biscuits (see page 229). We were tempted to try making them with choc chips (using the technique described on page 218). But unfortunately, the Chocolate Glaze can't be used as choc chips in baking due to its low melting temperature and runny texture. However, you can press a chip into the centre of each biscuit before baking. If you can't be bothered, these yummy biscuits work fine without the chips, too.

Makes approx. 20

120 g butter
¾ cup dextrose
2 eggs
vanilla essence
1½ cups self-raising flour
½ cup desiccated coconut
pinch of salt
Chocolate Glaze chips, if desired (see page 218)

1. Preheat oven to 180°C (350°F). Line a baking tray with paper.

2. Beat butter and dextrose to a cream.

3. Add eggs one at a time, beating well after each addition.

4. Add vanilla essence and mix through.

5. Sift flour into a separate bowl, then add coconut and salt.
6. Gradually mix dry ingredients into wet. (Be patient – drier mixtures take time to mix together.)
7. Roll mixture into dessertspoon-sized balls, pushing a Chocolate Glaze chip (if desired) into the centre of each. Place on prepared baking tray. They don't spread much but you should allow 1 cm or so between the edges.
8. Cook until starting to colour (15–20 minutes).
9. Cool biscuits on a wire rack.

Jaffa Biscuits

Kids love to take a treat for morning tea at school every now and then. These bikkies are not very sweet but still seem to be a hit. The bitterness of the cocoa cuts through any sweetness the dextrose adds and the strong orange scent makes for a winning combination. You can sweeten them up with the Chocolate Glaze if you like, but we don't bother.

Makes approx. 20

1 cup self-raising flour
1 cup dextrose
¾ cup plain flour
¼ cup cocoa
2 eggs, lightly beaten
150 g butter, melted
1 tablespoon finely grated orange rind

1. Preheat oven to 180°C (350°F). Line a baking tray with paper.
2. Sift dry ingredients together in a bowl.
3. Combine wet ingredients and orange rind, then mix into dry. (Be patient – the mixture should resemble biscuit crumbs but stick together when pressed. If it won't stick together, add a little more melted butter.)

4. Roll mixture into dessertspoon-sized balls and press gently onto prepared tray. They don't spread much but you should allow 1 cm or so between the edges.

5. Bake for about 20 minutes or until firming. Leave on tray to firm further before transferring to a wire rack.

Macadamia Nut Biscuits

These biscuits are a variation on the base biscuit mixture used in the Jaffa Biscuits (see page 227). If you prefer sweeter biscuits or fewer nuts, experiment a little to find your ideal recipe.

Makes approx. 12

½ cup self-raising flour
½ cup plain flour
½ cup dextrose
125 g macadamia nut pieces
1 egg, lightly beaten
100 g butter, melted and cooled
vanilla essence

1. Preheat oven to 180°C (350°F). Line a baking tray with paper.
2. Sift dry ingredients together in a bowl; add macadamia pieces.
3. Mix together egg, butter and vanilla essence.
4. Mix wet ingredients into dry (this is a moister mixture than the others).
5. Roll mixture into dessertspoon-sized balls and press gently onto lined oven tray
6. Bake for about 20 minutes.

Anzac Biscuits (Rolled-oat Biscuits)

A critical part of the traditional Anzac biscuit is golden syrup. Unfortunately, it's full of fructose, so it's not an option. This recipe does, however, get very close to the original taste and texture of an Anzac biscuit. It uses glucose syrup to obtain that nice hard finish you expect in an Anzac biscuit.

If, like me, you miss gingernut bikkies, try adding 2 teaspoons of ground ginger (or more, if you like) and 1 teaspoon of cinnamon to this mixture before you bake it.

Makes approx. 24

1 cup plain flour
1 cup rolled oats
¾ cup coconut
1¼ cups dextrose
150 g butter
3 tablespoons boiling water
4 tablespoons glucose syrup
1 teaspoon baking powder

1. Preheat oven to 150°C (300°F). Line two baking trays with paper.

2. Sift flour into a large bowl.

3. Add oats, coconut and dextrose, then set aside.

4. Melt butter in a saucepan, then add syrup and water. Allow mixture to boil briefly before taking off the heat.

5. Add baking powder to the saucepan, allow it to foam, then pour immediately onto dry ingredients. Mix well.

6. Take heaped-teaspoon-sized pieces of mixture and press out thinly (about a finger width) onto greased trays, allowing room for spreading.

7. Bake for approximately 30 minutes until golden.

8. Cool on a wire rack (biscuits will be soft and spongy when warm, but will harden as they cool).

Almond Bread

Almond bread has always been a favourite at our place. Before I broke my addiction, no Christmas would be complete without sugar-based, glazed, cherry-filled almond bread. This dextrose alternative might not satisfy real almond-bread aficionados (as there are no glacé cherries), but the texture and the taste still feel like Christmas to me.

Makes approx. 50 slices

3 egg whites
⅔ cup dextrose
⅔ cup plain flour, sifted
90 g unblanched almonds

1. Preheat oven to 160°C (325°F). Grease and line a log tin.

2. Whip egg whites until stiff.

3. Beat in dextrose gradually, a tablespoon at a time.

4. Fold in flour and almonds.

5. Put into prepared tin.

6. Bake for 45 minutes (but keep an eye on the bread after 30 minutes) until firm to touch and golden.

7. Turn out of tin and cool on a wire rack.

8. Once cold, carefully cut into very thin slices using a serrated bread knife (dextrose almond bread hardens more than the traditional version, so cut the slices as thinly as you can).

9. Lay the slices out flat on lined baking trays.

10. Cook in a slow oven (150°C/300°F) until just golden.

11. Turn over to colour the other side (be careful not to overcook; remember that the slices will not harden or crisp until they cool).

12. Place on a wire rack to cool and harden.

13. Store in an airtight container (this is especially important if you live in a humid environment – these things soak up water like a sponge).

Italian Meringue

Meringues are a little tricky without sugar but this recipe works brilliantly with dextrose. Keep in mind that dextrose seems to cook faster than sugar. It doesn't take long for the dextrose mixture on the stove to hit the soft 'ball' stage (where a drop of mixture forms a ball when put in cold water), and you must be careful not to leave it too long or the dextrose will burn. This also goes for the meringues while they are in your oven.

Lizzie has occasionally used this recipe to make flat macaroons by folding through some cocoa and shredded coconut. Others have used it to make ice-cream (make the Italian Meringue mix, then fold in some whipped cream and freeze it). Italian Meringue is also the base for the Italian Buttercream Icing (see page 219), which can be used to ice cakes.

If your meringues are a little sticky once they cool, put them back in the oven at the same temperature for a short while (no more than ½ hour) and then repeat the cooling-down process as before.

Makes approx. 30 small meringues

¾ cup dextrose
1 teaspoon glucose syrup
2 teaspoons water
2 egg whites

1. Preheat oven to 120°C (250°F). Line baking trays with paper.

2. Combine dextrose, syrup and water in a saucepan and dissolve over a gentle heat.

3. Increase heat and bring syrup to the boil.

4. Using an electric mixer, beat egg whites into soft peaks.

5. When the dextrose mixture is at soft ball stage (this takes very little time – only a few minutes), trickle it into the egg whites while still beating. Continue beating until whites are silky, stiff and very white (and until the mixture starts to cool).

6. Place small spoonfuls on prepared trays.

7. Bake for 2 hours (keep watch after 1½ hours to avoid burning) then turn off the oven, leaving the meringues inside only to the point of hardening. (Note that, unlike sugar meringues, these do not harden until they begin to cool.)

8. Store immediately in an airtight container

Desserts

No recipe guide about food for special occasions would be complete without lots of yummy desserts. Like some of the other recipes, some of these desserts will be best appreciated by fructose-free guests. Others will appeal to all comers.

Royal Raspberry Tart

Nothing beats a good tart. You can make it ahead of time and cover it in berries (just before you serve it) for that wow factor. You can also mix and match bases with the Baked Cheesecake (see page 234). Lizzie has used the cheesecake base with the tart filling when she's had to make a gluten-free dessert (the cheesecake base has less flour, so using gluten-free flour affects the taste less). She has also made individual tarts (great finger food for a party) by pressing the base into well-greased but unlined pattypan tins, then baking, cooling and filling them.

Serves 8–10

1 punnet raspberries (or any other berries you like)

COCONUT PASTRY
1 cup plain flour (scant)
1 cup shredded coconut (scant)
90 g butter
¼ cup dextrose
1 egg yolk

FILLING
¾ cup dextrose
2 tablespoons cornflour
1 tablespoon powdered gelatine
2 eggs plus 1 egg yolk
350 ml milk
vanilla essence (optional)
150 ml thickened cream

Prepare coconut pastry

1. Preheat oven to 180°C (350°F).
2. Combine all pastry ingredients, mixing with fingertips until just blended.
3. Press dough onto bottom and up sides of 25 cm (loose-bottomed if you have it) flan tin.
4. Prick pastry base with fork in several places to prevent shrinkage and puffing during baking.
5. Blind bake for 10 minutes (line pastry shell with foil then rice, dried beans or baking weights to stop pastry from lifting as it cooks).
6. Remove foil and weights and cook, uncovered, for a further 5–10 minutes until pastry begins to colour.
7. Cool on a wire rack while still in tin.

Prepare filling

1. Combine dextrose, cornflour and gelatine in medium saucepan.
2. Whisk together egg, egg yolk and milk.
3. Stir egg mix into gelatine mix.
4. Allow to stand for 5 minutes (to let gelatine soften).
5. Cook over a low heat, stirring constantly until the mixture thickens (this will happen suddenly).
6. Stir through vanilla essence if desired.
7. Once thickened, pour filling into a large bowl and refrigerate.
8. Stir the filling occasionally, waiting for it to cool and mound slightly when dropped from a spoon.
9. Whip the cream to stiff peaks.
10. Whisk or fold the cream into the filling.

Assemble

1. Carefully lift cooled coconut pastry case onto a serving platter.
2. Spoon filling into case.
3. Top with raspberries.
4. Refrigerate until filling is completely set (about 1 hour).

Baked Cheesecake

If you can't be bothered with the base for this cheesecake, pour the filling into eight large ramekins and bake them for 40–50 minutes or until firm to touch. It makes for a yummy single-serve dish (which also happens to be a gluten-free dessert).

The base mixture also makes a great topping for a fruit crumble (or see the nut-free version on page 238).

Serves 8–10

BASE

These quantities are only enough for a base. If you wish to do a base and sides, you will need a double quantity.

½ cup flaked almonds
½ cup dextrose
⅓ cup plain flour
⅔ cup coconut
50 g butter, melted (plus extra if needed)

FILLING
500 g cream cheese
1½ cups dextrose
1 tablespoon cornflour
3 eggs
vanilla essence
2 tablespoons lemon juice
pinch of salt
2 cups sour cream

Prepare base

1. Preheat oven to 180°C/350°F.
2. To make a springform tin watertight for a bain-marie, put foil over the base and through to the outside before snapping the tin in place. Grease foil inside tin.
3. Mix dry ingredients together in a bowl.
4. Rub in melted butter until mixture has a crumbly appearance and will just hold together.
5. Press mixture into base of prepared tin.
6. Bake until brown (approximately 10 mins); cool.

Prepare filling

1. Using an electric mixer, beat together the cheese and dextrose until smooth.
2. Beat in the cornflour.
3. Add eggs one at a time, beating well between each addition.
4. Add the vanilla essence, lemon juice, salt and sour cream, and beat briefly to combine.

Assemble

1. Pour filling onto prepared base.
2. Bake in bain-marie (place tin inside a baking dish and half-fill the baking dish with water) for 50 mins.
3. Turn off oven, but *do not* open oven door for a further 1 hour.
4. Chill and serve cold with cream or ice-cream.

No-bake Cheesecake

This recipe makes a cake about half the height of the Baked Cheesecake.

Serves 8–10

BASE

These quantities are only enough for a base. If you wish to do a base and sides, you will need a double quantity.

½ cup flaked almonds
½ cup dextrose
⅓ cup plain flour
⅔ cup coconut
50 g butter, melted (plus extra if needed)

FILLING

3 teaspoons powdered gelatine
250 g cream cheese
⅓ cup lemon juice
1 teaspoon lemon rind
¾ cup dextrose (or ½ cup if you prefer less sweetness)
250 ml cream, whipped

Prepare base

1. Preheat oven to 150°C (300°F). Line the base of a small (20 cm) springform tin with baking paper. Grease the sides and base of the tin well.
2. Mix dry ingredients together in a bowl.
3. Rub in melted butter until mixture has a crumbly appearance and will just hold together.
4. Press mixture into base of prepared tin (and up the sides if you have enough).
5. Bake in oven until golden (watch carefully – it should take about 10–15 minutes); cool.

Prepare filling

1. Heat some water in a small saucepan on the stove, then place a heat-proof bowl on top of the saucepan. Place two tablespoons hot water in the bowl.
2. Sprinkle gelatine over hot water in bowl and stir to dissolve. Remove from saucepan and cool.
3. Beat cream cheese, lemon juice, rind and dextrose for 4–5 minutes.
4. Add cooled gelatine.
5. Using a large metal spoon, fold whipped cream into cream cheese mixture.

Assemble

1. Pour filling into cooled base and refrigerate before serving.

Apple Pie

Obviously, this pie, with its eight large apples, is not fructose-free. But by retaining the apple skin, we at least ensure that everything that was in the apple (except perhaps some water) goes into the pie. Depending on how generous you are with your slices, a slice (one-eighth) of this pie is likely to be the equivalent of eating one apple, so no seconds for you.

This recipe can be used with all sorts of fruit (skin on) as well as combinations (apple and rhubarb or mulberry etc.).

Serves 8–10

PASTRY

1 cup self-raising flour
1 cup plain flour
2 tablespoons dextrose
155 g cold butter, chopped
1 egg, lightly beaten
3–4 tablespoons iced water
Egg and/or milk, for glaze

FILLING

8 large apples
¾ cup water
2 tablespoons cinnamon
2 tablespoons dextrose (vary according to the sweetness of the apples used; the recipe will even work without any dextrose, if the cupboard is bare)

Prepare pastry

2. Sift together flours and dextrose.
3. Add butter, rubbing in with fingertips until the mixture resembles breadcrumbs. Make a well in the centre.
4. Using a knife, stir in egg and enough iced water to bring dough together.
5. Press dough into a ball and refrigerate for 20 minutes.

Prepare filling

1. Core and slice apples (leaving the skin on).
2. Place apples in a saucepan with water, cinnamon and dextrose.

3. Cover and simmer until apples are tender but still firm enough to hold their shape.

4. Cool.

Assemble

1. Preheat oven to 180°C (350°F). Grease sides and base of a 24 cm pie dish.

2. Roll out two-thirds of the pastry dough and line the sides and base of the prepared dish. Refrigerate for 10 minutes.

3. Spoon the cooled apple mixture into the pastry.

4. Roll out the rest of the dough to make the pie top, reserving a little for decorations (whatever you like).

5. Brush decorated pie top with egg and/or milk glaze. Brush edge of pastry sides with glaze and place pie top over the apple mixture, pressing the sides and top together to seal.

6. Make several slits in top of pie for steam holes.

7. Bake for about 45 minutes or until golden and cooked through.

8. Serve with cream, dextrose ice-cream or custard.

Nut-free Crumble Topping

The beauty of crumble is that you can tweak the topping to suit your tastes, and the dessert only takes as long to cook as the fruit takes to warm and the crumble to brown.

Serves 6

1 cup quick oats
½ cup plain flour
½ cup coconut
⅓ cup dextrose
125 g butter, melted (plus extra if needed)

1. Mix dry ingredients together in a bowl.

2. Add butter and mix until topping is the consistency of sticky breadcrumbs (use more butter if required).

3. Sprinkle over stewed or fresh fruit of your choice in a ceramic pie dish, and bake until golden in a preheated oven at around 180°C (350°F).

Pannacotta

I love pannacotta. In fact, this is definitely my favourite dextrose dessert. I love the texture and the very subtle flavour. Unfortunately, sugarholics have a very different taste perception to those who aren't addicted; they can't distinguish shades and subtleties of flavour. This dessert may not be a sweet-enough treat for all sugarholic guests. For them, opt for the White-chocolate Bavarois (page 240), which is considerably sweeter tasting.

I have been reliably informed by Frank (a good friend who happens to have been born in Sicily), that this recipe produces pannacotta that tastes exactly the way it should. He says the majority of pannacotta made in Australia is far too sweet.

Serves 4

200 ml milk
300 ml thickened cream
1 vanilla bean
1½ teaspoons powdered gelatine
2 tablespoons warm water (for softening gelatine)
⅓ cup dextrose

1. Grease 4 single-serve (100 ml) jelly moulds and set aside.
2. Mix milk and cream in a saucepan.
3. Split vanilla bean, scrape out seeds and add both bean and seeds to the saucepan.
4. Heat gently over a low heat, stirring constantly. Bring almost to boiling point but don't let it boil. Remove saucepan from heat and take out vanilla bean (leave seeds).
5. Sprinkle gelatine over warm water and allow to soften.
6. Add softened gelatine to saucepan, whisking until it is completely dissolved.

7. Cool in the fridge for ½ hour.
8. Stir mixture to ensure vanilla seeds are well distributed.
9. Pour into jelly moulds and set in the fridge (allow several hours minimum).
10. Serve with berries rather than ice-cream, as the sweetness of (even dextrose) ice-cream will overwhelm the subtle flavour and texture.

White-chocolate Bavarois

Although there is no white chocolate in this recipe, the sweetness is so reminiscent (of what I think I remember it tastes like!) that I decided to name it that way. It is not really a 'bavarois' either, because it has no eggs. But to my sugar-free tastebuds, it tastes magnificently like white-chocolate bavarois.

Serves 6

1 cup milk
2 cups thickened cream
1 cup dextrose
1 vanilla bean
1 tablespoon powdered gelatine
3 tablespoons warm water (for softening gelatine)

1. Grease 6 single-serve (100 ml) jelly moulds and set aside.
2. Heat milk, cream, dextrose and vanilla bean (split) over medium heat, almost bringing to the boil.
3. Sprinkle gelatine over water and allow to soften.
4. Whisk gelatine into cream mixture on stove, allowing it to simmer for 4 minutes.
5. Strain then pour into greased moulds.
6. Refrigerate for 4–6 hours or until set.

Passionfruit Delight

This started out as a soufflé recipe but, while it does rise (and therefore must be served immediately), it doesn't rise as much as you might expect. So, in the interests of managing expectations, I've changed its name.

The recipe contains passionfruit juice, which is about 5 per cent fructose – so the dessert in total will deliver 1.5g of fructose. This results in an insignificant amount of fructose per serving, even though it has no compensating fibre.

Serves 4

1 teaspoon butter
2 eggs, separated
⅓ cup dextrose + 2 tablespoons extra
30 ml passionfruit juice, strained
Pinch of salt

1. Preheat oven to 180°C (350°F). Grease 4 large (150 ml) ramekins with butter and sprinkle with the extra dextrose (2 tablespoons).
2. Cream egg yolks with half the dextrose until pale (and the dextrose is dissolved).
3. Add juice; mix and set aside.
4. In a separate bowl, whisk egg whites with salt. Before peaks form, add half the remaining dextrose, whisk, then add remaining half. Beat the mix until stiff peaks appear.
5. Whisk one-third of the whites into the yolks then carefully add the rest.
6. Place ramekins in a bain-marie (sit them all in a baking dish and half-fill the dish with water), and bake for 12–15 minutes until coloured and risen slightly. Serve immediately.

Vanilla Soufflé

This is the real deal: a gloriously puffy soufflé. You can use a single soufflé dish rather than ramekins if you prefer, but allow about twice the baking time. The bain-marie is not critical, but we've found that with soufflés containing flour, you avoid a crusty base if you use one.

Serves 4

30 g butter + 1 teaspoon extra
¼ cup dextrose + 2 tablespoons extra
3 tablespoons flour
1 cup milk
vanilla essence
3 egg yolks
4 egg whites

1. Preheat oven to 180°C (350°F). Grease 4 large (150 ml) ramekins with the extra butter (1 teaspoon) and sprinkle with the extra dextrose (2 tablespoons).
2. Melt butter and stir in flour, cooking gently.
3. Add milk, stirring until the mixture boils and thickens.
4. Stir in dextrose and vanilla essence. Remove from heat and allow to cool.
5. Beat in egg yolks.
6. In a separate bowl, whisk egg whites until stiff. Fold into vanilla mixture.
7. Pour mixture into prepared ramekins.
8. Place ramekins in a bain-marie (sit them all in a baking dish and half-fill the dish with water) and bake for 30 minutes or until risen and golden. (Be gentle removing the soufflé from the oven – you don't want it to lose its puff.)

Breakfast

Man cannot live on Vegemite toast or bacon and eggs alone. Here's a couple of ideas for some variety at the breakfast table.

Pancakes

Pancakes are a specialty of my 10-year-old daughter. She loves whipping up a batch on the weekend. Her biggest challenge is keeping everyone else away from them long enough to create a visually pleasing stack.

Serves 6 (Gillespie) kids – your mileage may vary

2 cups self-raising flour
¼ cup dextrose
1 teaspoon baking powder
1½ cups milk
3 eggs, lightly beaten
½ teaspoon vanilla essence
pinch of salt
50 g butter, melted and cooled

1. Sift dry ingredients together in a bowl.
2. Mix wet ingredients (except butter) together in a large jug.
3. Add dry ingredients and butter to the jug and mix. Don't stir too much; it doesn't matter if it's lumpy.
4. Put a greased frying pan on a moderate heat and wait until it reaches a high temperature.
5. Pour batter to size of pancake required.
6. Cook until bubbles form on top of pancake, then flip and cook other side.
7. Press the top of the pancake with your finger. If it bounces back rather than leaving a depression, it's ready.
8. Serve with butter or sprinkle with dextrose and berries. These would also go well under a poached egg with Simple Hollandaise Sauce (see page 205).

Phillips Family Muesli

The nuts in this recipe contain trace amounts of fructose but also dish up truly massive amounts of fibre. The recipe also happens to be gluten-free. Once again, thanks to the Phillips family for this recipe.

Makes approx. 10–14 serves

1 cup roasted unsalted peanuts
1 cup macadamia nuts
1 cup walnuts
¼ cup sunflower seeds
¼ cup desiccated coconut
3 cups rolled oats

1. Process the nuts in a blender for a couple of blasts so most are crushed but some remain whole.

2. In a large, lidded airtight container, mix the nuts in with the other ingredients, shaking (lid on unless you like using a broom) until you achieve a uniform consistency.

3. Serve with cold milk and/or natural yoghurt, and even some chopped-up fruit. Or, if you prefer, microwave muesli and milk for a nice hot brekkie.

Notes

Throughout the book, you'll have noticed case studies from various people. These are drawn (with permission) directly from comments that these people have posted in the free online forum that I maintain at http://sweetpoison.myfreeforum.org/index.php. The posts may have been edited for grammar (Penguin editors are like that) but they are pretty much intact. The really great thing is that if you want to ask any questions about the case studies, all you need to do is log on to the forum and ask the person directly. You gotta love that internet!

Introduction

Distressingly, those we entrust to look after our health appear to have given up on getting us off sugar before they even try. This is from the *Dietary Guidelines for Australian Adults 2003* (page 186), available at nhmrc.gov.au/_files_nhmrc/file/publications/synopses/n33.pdf:

'. . . moderate use of sugars as sweeteners or to add flavour may actually improve the palatability of food and increase overall nutrient consumption'

And this:

'A diet without any sugar would be impractical, hence this guideline: "Consume only moderate amounts of sugars and foods containing added sugars".'

1. Sweet poison

The source for **Figure 1.1** is Noel Deer's 1949 epic, *The History of Sugar* (Chapman & Hall). I have converted the historical prices to approximate equivalent values in Australian dollars.

Unless I say otherwise in this chapter, the statistics on obesity are US-based. The US is the only reliable source for historical population obesity data that stretches this far back in time.

The medical textbook which observed that people eat more when they exercise more was *Obesity and Leanness* by Hugo R. Rony (published by Lea & Febiger in Philadelphia, 1940).

The joint guideline on physical activity published by the American Heart Association and the American College of Sports Medicine in August 2007 [medscape.com/viewarticle/561348] reviewed all the available evidence. It recommended that 30 minutes of moderate physical activity five days a week is necessary to 'promote and maintain health'. Noticeably absent from the guideline is any suggestion that exercise will definitely lead to any weight reduction. The best it could come up with is:

'It is reasonable to assume that persons with relatively high daily energy expenditures would be less likely to gain weight over time, compared with those who have low energy expenditures. So far, data to support this hypothesis are not particularly compelling . . .'

The data in **Figure 1.2** are sourced from the US Centers for Disease Control NHANES Surveys [cdc.gov/nchs/nhanes.htm] for the numbers after 1960. For the 1870 numbers, I used the Union Army data set [cpe.uchicago.edu/unionarmy/unionarmy.html].

The numbers for Australian obesity come from the excellent reports prepared by the federal government's Australian Institute of Health and Welfare [http://www.aihw.gov.au/publications/gep/gpaia98-99-07-08-10ydt/gpaia98-99-07-08-10ydt-c14.pdf].

The data on how much each of us exercises come from the annual *Exercise, Recreation and Sport Survey* prepared by the Australian Sport Commission [ausport.gov.au/information/scors/ERASS/exercise,_recreation_and_sport_survey_past_reports/erass_2008].

The data on sports equipment sales in the US come courtesy of SGMA, the trade association of leading industry sports and fitness brands [sgma.com/press/3/U.S.-Sports-Industry:-Nearly-a-$70-Billion-Business].

If you like reading about nasty things happening to rats fed fructose, then this study is a good place to start: *Fructose-induced metabolic syndrome is associated with glomerular hypertension and renal microvascular damage in rats* [ajprenal.physiology.org/cgi/content/abstract/292/1/F423?ijkey=673f17fd19cb402ec40ee5b6e7215f17e1359c44&keytype2=tf_ipsecsha].

Figure 1.3 was created by merging data from the US Department of Agriculture's (USDA) food consumption databases [ers.usda.gov/data/FoodConsumption/] since 1909 and Union Army data set (see above) for prior to that date.

The source of the data on calorie consumption is the USDA food disappearance databases [ers.usda.gov/Data/FoodConsumption/

FoodGuideIndex.htm]. Disappearance is not an accurate measure of how much a population actually eats because it doesn't take into account the fact that two-year-olds only eat half of what's on their plate (and other less serious forms of wastage). But in terms of trends of consumption, it is a good proxy for how much people are eating in general, assuming wastage is always approximately the same percentage of consumption.

The statistics on diabetes in the US come from *Full Accounting of Diabetes and Pre-Diabetes in the U.S. Population in 1988–1994 and 2005–2006* [care.diabetesjournals.org/content/32/2/287.abstract].

The study about a bunch (should that be flock?) of Swedish twins is *Mid- and Late-Life Diabetes in Relation to the Risk of Dementia – A Population-Based Twin Study* [diabetes.diabetesjournals.org/content/58/1/71.full].

The data on the number of Australians with Alzheimer's disease comes from *Keeping Dementia Front of Mind: Incidence and prevalence 2009–2050*, prepared by Access Economics for Alzheimer's Australia [alzheimers.org.au/upload/Front_of_Mind_Full_Report1.pdf].

The impaired cognitive function study is entitled *Relationship Between Baseline Glycemic Control and Cognitive Function in Individuals with Type 2 Diabetes and Other Cardiovascular Risk Factors* and can be found online at care.diabetesjournals.org/content/32/2/221.full.

A summary of the Stanford School of Medicine study on the relationship between breast cancer and cortisol can be found online at med.stanford.edu/ism/2009/august/depression.html.

Surprise! Sugar is addictive

An abstract of the Princeton study is available online at sciencedirect.com/science?_ob=ArticleURL&_udi=B6T0J-4NS0KSK-1&_user=10&_coverDate=12/31/2008&_rdoc=1&_fmt=high&_orig=search&_sort=d&_docanchor=&view=c&_

searchStrId=1202650230&_rerunOrigin=scholar.
google&_acct=C000050221&_version=1&_urlVer-
sion=0&_userid=10&md5=63823204f76aea7a9e57f79da
ea38d0a, and the Duke study at http://www.sciencedirect.
com/science?_ob=ArticleURL&_udi=B6WSS-4S4SJTX-J&_
user=10&_rdoc=1&_fmt=&_orig=search&_sort=d&view=c&_
acct=C000050221&_version=1&_urlVersion=0&_userid=10&md
5=b1b01f1faa22e884d61d9e2b72b1c055. If you want to read the
full version of either of these (go on, you know you do) you'll need
to get your wallet out.

Gardening is pleasurable (for some people, at least) and, like
anything pleasurable, it does stimulate a dopamine response. But
it is a brief spike – your dopamine receptors are not suppressed (as
they are with amphetamines and fructose) and your opioid receptors are not increased. So the pleasure is there, but it is passing
rather than addictive.

Traci Mann's review of calorie restricting diets can be found at
http://psycnet.apa.org/index.cfm?fa=buy.optionToBuy&id=
2007-04834-008&CFID=5232229&CFTOKEN=21444842.

2. How to break the addiction
Step 3 Eliminating sugar

If you'd like to read more about Nutrition Information Panels (and
food labelling in general), Food Standards Australia and New Zealand have prepared a very thorough explanation that is available at
foodstandards.gov.au/consumerinformation/foodlabelling/.

The '10 lowest-sugar' and '10 highest-sugar' tables of foods
and their sugar content should be taken with a grain of salt (pun
intended). They are based on a point-in-time review of the products
on the shelves of my local supermarket. I have not examined every
single brand of every single item of food. They are intended as a

guide to the types of each kind of food that are likely to be low (or high) in sugar. You should always read the labels to check the sugar content yourself. But these tables should at least help to narrow the number of items you need to check. I have published the complete lists from which these tables are drawn. You can find them online at howmuchsugar.com

One of the more recent studies on the benefits or otherwise of vitamins is the *Mortality in Randomized Trials of Antioxidant Supplements for Primary and Secondary Prevention – Systematic Review and Meta-analysis*; it can be found at jama.ama-assn.org/cgi/content/full/297/8/842.

Many of the lists I provide for general categories of food where I don't name a specific product are based on publicly available nutrient databases. Some of the best ones are:

- **NUTTAB** is Food Standards Australia and New Zealand's online database of nutrient values. It contains data for approximately 2600 foods and up to 169 nutrients: foodstandards.gov.au/consumerinformation/nuttab2006/onlineversionintroduction/
- **Fineli** is a similar database maintained by Finland's National Institute of Health and Welfare: fineli.fi/index.php?lang=en
- The US Department of Agriculture maintains a similarly extensive database online: nal.usda.gov/fnic/foodcomp/search/

If you match one food across each of those databases, you may well get different values for sugar content. This reflects the fact that there is no such thing as a standard apple or grape or carrot. There will be variation (often large) from region to region in terms of sugar content. In the comparative charts in chapter 2, I've tried to strike an average value for foods in each category. But, for this reason, the charts are best for comparing relative amounts rather than being definitive about the exact amount of sugar in the food you hold in your hand.

Two of the recent studies on the potential beneficial effects of alcohol are: *Alcohol and Cardiovascular Health* [content.onlinejacc.org/cgi/content/abstract/50/11/1009] and *Beneficial Postprandial Effect of a Small Amount of Alcohol on Diabetes and Cardiovascular Risk Factors: Modification by Insulin Resistance* [jcem.endojournals.org/cgi/content/abstract/90/2/661].

Step 4 – Withdrawal

In 'Going cold turkey' (p.87), I say that you can't afford to have any fructose after you start withdrawal. It looks (from my mailbag) like this will not necessarily be the same for everyone. The amount you can have without turning the cravings on seems to differ from person to person. Some people can have a square of chocolate every day and be fine, while others (like me) can't have any.

Men are from Mars

Dr MacDonald's study of the difference between male and female fructose consumption is available online at ajcn.org/cgi/reprint/18/5/369, and the Lausanne University study that affirms the findings is available at care.diabetesjournals.org/content/31/6/1254.full.

Dr Krauss has published extensively in the area of LDL particle size research. You'll can get a full list of his publications from chori.org/Principal_Investigators/Krauss_Ronald/krauss_pubs.html. The full text of the study relating fructose consumption and LDL particle size in Swiss school children is available online at ajcn.org/cgi/content/full/86/4/1174.

Which fruit?

The Australian Guide to Healthy Eating is available in full online at health.gov.au/internet/healthyactive/publishing.nsf/Content/eating (in case you want to see how much fruit they say you should eat).

Butter and margarine

The write-up of John Yudkin's experiment with 11 people is available at ajcn.org/cgi/reprint/23/7/948. Ancel Keys' study on 36 people isn't available online unless you have a subscription to the *British Medical Bulletin*. (If you do, here's the link: bmb.oxfordjournals.org/cgi/reprint/8/4/395-b.)

3. Meal planner

Just in case any McDonald's lawyers are reading this, I have published their menus as an example because they are one of the few fast-food outlets that make detailed nutritional information available. These lists are just a reformatting of the lists published by McDonald's themselves. If you would prefer to read the originals, you can get them from mcdonalds.com.au/our-food/nutrition.

What's for lunch, Mum and Dad?

The UK schoolchildren study is available in the *British Medical Journal* online at bmj.com/cgi/content/full/328/7450/1237.

The Yale University study (on kids and breakfast cereals) does not yet appear to have been published in a journal, but you can download a summary from the researchers at cerealfacts.org/media/Sugar_Cereal_Study.pdf.

4. What on earth is that?

The three studies I mention on the potential downsides to artificial sweeteners are:

- *Diet Soda Intake and Risk of Incident Metabolic Syndrome and Type 2 Diabetes in the Multi-Ethnic Study of Atherosclerosis (MESA)* [care.diabetesjournals.org/content/32/4/688.full]
- *Dietary Intake and the Development of the Metabolic Syndrome: The Atherosclerosis Risk in Communities Study* [circ.ahajournals.org/cgi/content/full/116/5/480?ijkey=8d5 08adefbc35e188bb26910699194c845c4fc78]
- *Soft Drink Consumption and Risk of Developing Cardiometabolic Risk Factors and the Metabolic Syndrome in Middle-aged Adults in the Community* [circ.ahajournals.org/cgi/content/full/116/5/480?ijkey=8d508adefbc35e188bb2691069919 4c845c4fc78]

The abstract for Susan Swithers' and Terry Davidson's rat study is available at psycnet.apa.org/index.cfm?fa=buy.optionToBuy&id= 2008-01943-017&CFID=6120165&CFTOKEN=71116537, but if you want to read the full thing, you'll need to find $11.95.

5. Recipes

You're looking for notes about recipes? C'mon, get real. Fire up the oven, start cooking and make your own notes!

Acknowledgements

Having only just mastered boiling water and toasting bread, I was in no position to write a book that contained recipes of any description, let alone recipes requiring experimentation with a weird new ingredient. I am therefore deeply indebted to the efforts of my lovely wife, Lizzie (and our crew of six taste-testers), who stepped up in a very big way. Lizzie spent six months building, trying, failing, trying and eventually succeeding in making sure these recipes work. And for that extreme persistence, attention to detail and dedication to the sugar-free life we are building for our family, I am very grateful.

Besides the kids, we had an army of valiant taste-testers who all deserve recognition for munching their way through (what must have seemed like) endless samples from the Gillespie kitchen. Tatjana in the tuckshop inspired Lizzie and stuck with her on the tasting rounds. Beth went further, trying out variations of her own and even occasionally administering them to her sugar-lovin' hubby (without complete disclosure). And Melinda and Susan (and their families) often found it difficult to escape the school grounds without having a muffin or meringue forced on them for critical evaluation.

I try to avoid banging on about sugar to those who have to put up with me on an extended basis. So it came as a bit of a surprise when Darren Phillips (an American chap I help mess about with computers) lobbed up with his recipes for Ketchup and Muesli. He'd quietly been moving his family to sugarlessness but had hit a problem when it came to these two essential items. He's a detailed kind of bloke, so he set to the task of making both without sugar. The results were so good that I demanded his permission to put them in this book.

Before *Sweet Poison* hit the streets, I was telling the story of a single case study (me). Now, thousands of people have started a sugar-free life. Many of those people share their experiences on the *Sweet Poison* public discussion forums (located at http://sweetpoison. myfreeforum.org/index.php). Koboli, Vicki J, Mikedufty, AJ, Raegose, Marita, Wise23girl, Lani, Paul and Bushturkey have all been regular contributors. I am very grateful for their many insightful comments and tips online, and especially for the stories they have agreed to share with us in this book.

Ingrid Ohlsson at Penguin decided *Sweet Poison* only told half the story. So it is thanks to her demand for completion that you hold the rest of the story in your hands today. Frank, as always, took care of the 'business stuff', as well as being the primary taste-tester for the pannacotta (his Italian heritage came into its own).

Nicci Dodanwela took the usual fact-checking fanaticism of Penguin editors and took it to a whole new level. If this book was a smooth (and accurate) reading experience, then it is entirely down to her diligence. If it wasn't, then it's her fault, too.

Index